unit 4

YOUR PERSONALITY AND YOUR HEART   77

unit 5

CULTURAL CHANGE: THE ANASAZI   113

appendix

Preface

Better Listening Skills is a series of five lectures on audiotape or videotape, accompanied by a student workbook and teacher's manual. The package helps the intermediate-level ESL student develop the necessary listening skills to understand segments of spoken English that are longer than those in simple daily conversation.

Each unit is a self-contained lesson. Together the units form a carefully sequenced program that teaches the student to listen for both factual details and organizational structure. The total program can be used as an important part of a listening comprehension or study skills course, since it also includes reading and writing practice.

The student workbook is an indispensable part of the listening program. The workbook makes it possible for students to begin this kind of lecture listening very early in their program of English study. Each lecture is supported by an unusually rich number and variety of exercises to prepare, to involve, and to reinforce the student for each listening experience. Students at the intermediate level of English study should find the lectures challenging but not too difficult to understand with the help of the exercises. The topics have been selected to hold student interest. They range across a wide spectrum of academic fields: space technology, energy research, economics, medicine, and cultural anthropology. The program has been successfully used with both college-bound and non–college-bound students, and both kinds of English learners have benefited from it. *Better Listening Skills* can be used with any English learner who plans to use the language in work or studies; it can aid in understanding lectures, television and radio programs, movies, and verbal instructions.

ACKNOWLEDGMENTS

We would like to acknowledge help received from various persons and agencies in the preparation of this series. The National Aeronautics and Space Administration was most helpful in providing both information and pictures for the Landsat unit. Mr. John Bayless of Solaron Corporation, Denver, Colorado, provided diagrams and explanations of solar-heated buildings for the second unit. The third lecture, "Barter: An Old Idea with New Power," was written and delivered on videotape by James A. Wills, economist. For the lecture about heart disease, "Your Personality and Your Heart," we thank most warmly Mr. Ronald Engler and Dr. Edward Machle for playing the parts of Adam and Bert, respectively. Thanks also go to Robin Elizabeth Machle, Catherine Michelle Machle Cabarga, and Jill Peterson, the children in the pictures. Finally, in gathering materials to illustrate the fifth lecture, "Cultural Change: The Anasazi," we received help from many sources. The Museums at Aztec National Monument and Mesa Verde National Park allowed us to use pictures of their ruins and artifacts. Photographers who donated their time most generously in the production of pictures were Stuart Wier and Joel Leigh Peterson.

For help in field testing and for creative criticism and suggestions, we also want to thank Ms. Mary Menogue and Ms. Marjorie Morray. For general support and professional encouragement during the writing of this project, we thank Ms. Jean Engler, director of the Intensive English Center at the University of Colorado.

JEAN SIMS
PATRICIA WILCOX PETERSON

Landsats:
Hope of the Future

INTRODUCTION TO THE LECTURE

Topic: Landsat Satellites

The Landsat satellites are two spacecraft in orbit around the earth. They photograph every part of the earth, except the North and South Poles, every nine days.

Thesis: Landsat Information Can Help Improve Our World

Through the photographs sent from the satellites, we are learning more about the earth than we have ever known before. This information can help us solve some of our current technological problems.

Organizational Strategy: Generalizations and Supporting Examples

The lecturer uses rhetorical questions to emphasize main topics. Rhetorical questions are questions that do not require an answer from the listener. Rather, the speaker answers his or her own question. Notice the use of rhetorical questions as topic headings in the outline.

Figure 1. Landsat satellite.

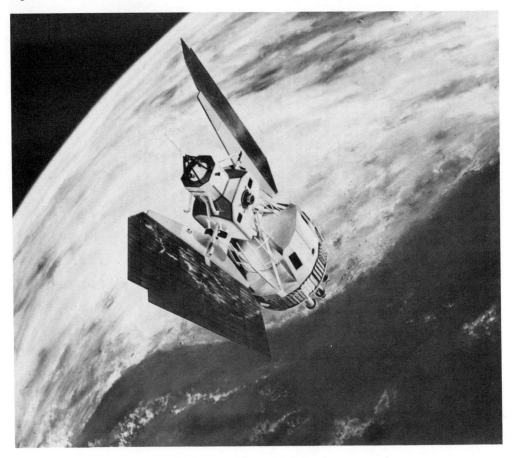

Photograph courtesy of National Aeronautics and Space Administration.

    I. Introduction
   II. What are Landsats?
  III. How do Landsats work?
  IV. How can Landsats be used?
   V. What are the future plans for Landsats?

BASIC SENTENCES

Directions: *Together the basic sentences provide a short summary of the main ideas in the lecture. Read and study these sentences be-before you listen to the lecture for the first time.*

1. The Landsats are two butterfly-shaped spacecraft that were sent into orbit around the earth in 1972 and 1975.

2. They photograph every part of the earth, except the North and South Poles, every nine days.

3. A Landsat photo is printed from black-and-white negatives through color filters to produce a false-color picture.

4. Scientists base their interpretations on the patterns of these colors rather than through observation of individual objects.

5. The first important use of these pictures is to create better maps.

6. The second use of these pictures is to help find oil and minerals.

7. Another use for the pictures is to find fresh water.

8. The fourth use is to warn us of natural disasters.

9. The fifth use is to watch crops growing around the world.

10. Future Landsats will be able to measure heat, photograph smaller areas, or search the earth with radar.

ADDITIONAL VOCABULARY

Directions: *Below are some additional words that may be new to you. Look up the ones you don't know before listening to the lecture.*

accurate	evolve	radar
barren	forest fire	rice
concentration	irrigate	satellite
corn	patch	soybeans
earthquake	pollution	sprinkler
		wheat

Listening Cues: Vocabulary of Numerical Order

Directions: *As you listen to the lecture, these words will help you understand the relationship of different ideas to one another.*

first	another	fifth
second	fourth	

STUDY SKILLS

The Standard Topic Outline Form

Outlining is a skill that will be useful to you when you are taking lecture notes, reading, or writing a paper. An outline shows the organization of a lecture or a written article. It is an organized list of ideas, grouped together in such a way as to show their relationship to one another.

We generally use a system of Roman numerals, Arabic numbers, and letters to show relationships. There is a standard form for using symbols to show which ideas are most important. The symbols used, in order of decreasing importance, are Roman numerals, capital letters, Arabic numbers, lower-case letters, and numbers in parentheses. The placement of the topics on the paper is important also, with the most important items farthest to the left. Lesser items are entered farther and farther to the right.

The blank form looks like this:

I. _____

    A. _____

    B. _____

    C. _____

II. _____

    A. _____

        1. _____

            a. _____

            b. _____

                (1) _____

                (2) _____

        2. _____

    B. _____

The letters and numbers are placed about three spaces to the right of the item above. Periods are used after Roman numerals and numbers. Headings of equal importance are indented an equal distance from the left margin (notice II. 1. and II. 2). The purpose of this indentation is to make each idea easy to see and to show just how it is related to the ideas before and after it. No punctuation is needed at the end of an idea unless it is written as a complete sentence.

Some students may already be familiar with a type of outline that uses the decimal system. This outline form shows the relationship between ideas by giving a decimal rank to each idea.

1. _____

   1.1 _____

   1.2 _____

2. _____

   2.1 _____

      2.11 _____

      2.12 _____

   2.2 _____

If you know how to use the decimal system well already, you can use it throughout the rest of this listening series. If not, we suggest you learn the standard topic outline form as shown on the previous page.

STUDY SKILLS

Exercise One: Classification

Outlining is a method of classifying and organizing ideas. In order to outline, you must understand how facts or ideas are related to one another. Study the two lists of information below.

To create better maps

To find fresh water

To find oil

To watch crops growing

To warn of natural disasters

To find large schools of fish

I. Uses for Landsats

    A. To create better maps
    B. To find fresh water
    C. To find oil
    D. To watch crops growing
    E. To warn of natural disasters
    F. To find large schools of fish

(Notice that the grammatical form of each topic is parallel.)

The list at the left contains the same information as the list at the right. But the list at the right is organized in a more meaningful way. The outlined list shows us the relationship of the topic to the lecture as a whole.

Practice: Organize the list on the left into outline form.

Chile

Water is black.

Canada

Rock is brown.

Brazil

Diseased plants are green.

Healthy plants are red.

Italy

Iran

I. A Landsat photo is printed through color filters to produce a false-color picture.

    A. _____

    B. _____

    C. _____

    D. _____

II. Other countries will receive Landsat data.

    A. _____

B. _____

C. _____

D. _____

E. _____

Exercise Two: Classification

In order to classify ideas together correctly, you need to know which ideas are related and which are not. In the following exercise, three words in each line are related and one is not. Decide what the related words have in common. Circle the one word that is not related to the others.

1. photograph   picture   print   (variety)
2. pattern   blue-green   black   brown
3. accurate   observation   correct   exact
4. Cape Cod   Cape Hatteras Cape Kennedy   South Dakota
5. provide   rotate   circle   orbit
6. crops   disaster   plants   trees
7. wheat   soybeans   acres   corn
8. fires   earthquakes   concentration storms
9. recognize   launch   observe   identify

Exercise Three: Recognizing Main Topics and Subtopics

Below is a list of sentences in random order about Landsat satellites. First, read all the sentences. Look for the best way they can be organized into an outline. Then copy each sentence on the appropriate line in the blank outline.

The Landsats are two butterfly-shaped spacecraft.
The second use is to find oil and minerals.
Scientists base their interpretations on the patterns of the colors.

How do Landsats work?

The first important use is to create better maps.

They were sent into orbit in 1972 and 1975.

How can Landsats be used?

A photo is printed from a black-and-white negative through color filters to produce a false-color picture.

What are Landsats?

Another use is to find fresh water.

I. _____

    A. _____

    B. _____

II. _____

    A. _____

    B. _____

III. _____

    A. _____

    B. _____

    C. _____

Exercise Four: Main Ideas and Supporting Details

Factual writing in English is usually organized in a series of main ideas and supporting details. Notice the organization of the following paragraph from the lecture:

> Another use for Landsat is to find fresh water. In dry areas such as deserts, Landsat photos may show black areas that indicate water or they may show red areas that indicate healthy plants.

Name: _____ Date: _____   **9**

I. Another use for Landsat is to find fresh
water. (main idea)

  A. In Landsat photos, black areas show
water. (supporting idea)
  B. Red areas show healthy plants. (supporting idea)

Here is another sample paragraph. Find the main idea and supporting details.

The fifth use is to warn us of natural disasters, such as the damage done by large forest fires, melting ice near the North and South Poles, and lines in the earth where earthquakes might happen.

I. _____ (main idea)

  _____

  A. _____ (supporting idea)

    _____

  B. _____ (supporting idea)

    _____

  C. _____ (supporting idea)

    _____

INCOMPLETE OUTLINE

Directions: *Read the outline before you listen to the lecture for the first time, so you will know what you need to listen for. While you are listening, find the missing dates and phrases to complete the outline. Mark your paper while you listen.*

  I. Introduction
  II. What are Landsats?

A. Two butterfly-shaped spacecraft sent into orbit in

_____ and _____.

B. They circle the earth _____ times every

_____ hours.

C. They photograph every part of the earth every

_____ days.

D. Each picture covers an area of about _____ square miles.

III. How do Landsats work?

A. A photo is printed from black-and-white negatives through color filters to produce a false-color picture.

1. Water is _____ .

2. _____ is brown.

3. Healthy plants are _____.

4. Diseased plants are _____.

B. Scientists base their interpretation on the patterns of the colors.

IV. How can Landsats be used?

A. The first important use is to create better _____.

B. The second use is to find _____.

C. Another use is to find _____.

D. The fourth use is to _____.

E. The fifth use is to _____.

F. Some other uses are:

    1. To find _____

    2. To show where _____

    3. To provide a record of _____

V. What are the future plans for Landsats?

    A. Another Landsat will measure _____.

    B. Other Landsats may be equipped with _____.
    C. Other countries that will receive Landsat data are:

        1. Canada
        2. Brazil
        3. Italy

        4. _____
        5. Zaire

        6. _____

WORD RECOGNITION EXERCISE

Directions: *Fill the blanks in each word family by finding the missing parts of speech in your dictionary. Divide each word into syllables and mark the syllable that takes the primary stress, as shown.*

Word Families

Noun	Verb	Adjective	Adverb
1. pos si bil´i ty	XXXXXXX	_____	_____
2. _____	e volve´	XXXXXXX	XXXXXXX
3. _____	_____	ob serv´a ble	_____

4. cre á tion   _____   _____   _____

5. _____   _____   pop'u la ted   XXXXXXX

6. _____   XXXXXXX   _____   ac'cu rate ly

7. _____   con'cen trate   _____   XXXXXXX

8. _____   _____   _____   i den ti fi'a bly

9. _____   _____   for'ma tive   XXXXXXX

10. in for má tion   _____   _____   XXXXXXX

11. _____   rep re sent'   _____   _____

12. de vel'op ment   _____   _____   XXXXXXX

13. _____   _____   in ter'pret a ble   XXXXXXX

14. _____   in'di cate   _____   XXXXXXX

TRUE-FALSE EXERCISE

Directions: *Read these sentences before you listen to the lecture for the second time. While you are listening, decide whether each item is true or false. Mark your paper with a T for true or an F for false while you listen.*

_____ 1. Landsats take pictures of every part of the earth.

_____ 2. The colors in Landsat photos do not look like colors in ordinary photos.

_____ 3. Maps made from pictures taken from airplanes are better than maps made from Landsat photos.

Name: _____   Date: _____   **13**

_____ 4. Landsat photos can show the kinds of rocks that indicate underground oil sources.

_____ 5. Fresh water is blue-green on Landsat maps.

_____ 6. In Landsat pictures you can tell the difference between corn and wheat growing in fields.

_____ 7. In these photos scientists can see lines in the earth where earthquakes might happen.

_____ 8. The Landsats, by counting people, show how the population of the world is growing.

_____ 9. Future Landsats will photograph larger areas.

_____ 10. You can buy a Landsat picture.

TOPICS FOR DISCUSSION AND WRITING

1. Do you think the Landsat spacecraft should be allowed to photograph other countries? How do you feel about the Landsats photographing your country?

2. How could your country use Landsat pictures? Which particular use of Landsat photos would be most important?

3. James C. Fletcher of NASA said that the Landsats are likely to save the world. Why do you think he said this?

4. Suppose Landsat photos show that the area of ice at the North and South Poles is becoming smaller. What might it mean? How could you use this information?

5. The lecturer states that people may purchase a variety of pictures for their own use. Do you think that the average person would have any trouble interpreting these pictures?

6. Imagine a situation like this: The Seasat satellite sends back information that there are waves 50 to 60 feet high in an area of the Pacific Ocean between Hawaii and Japan. How might this information be used?

7. Find these places on a map of the United States: Cape Cod, Long Island, New York City, Delaware Bay, Chesapeake Bay, Cape Hatteras, Cape Kennedy, Lake Okeechobee, Miami, the

Great Lakes, the Mississippi River, the Missouri River, the Great Salt Lake. Point the places out to your classmates.

MULTIPLE CHOICE EXERCISE

Directions: *Choose the one answer that best completes each sentence. Write the letter of the correct answer in the blank.*

_____ 1. A Landsat photo is printed from
     a. black-and-white negatives.
     b. color negatives.
     c. false-color negatives.
     d. none of the above.

_____ 2. In false-color pictures, water is
     a. red.
     b. black.
     c. white.
     d. blue-green.

_____ 3. From a height of 570 miles, _____ can be seen.
     a. automobiles
     b. people
     c. patches of color
     d. trees

_____ 4. If you wanted to look for water in the desert, you might look in Landsat photos for
     a. black areas.
     b. red areas.
     c. white areas.
     d. both black areas and red areas.

_____ 5. Which of the following could *not* be seen in a Landsat picture?
     a. damage done by large forest fires
     b. schools of fish
     c. pollution
     d. the number of animals in an area

Name: _____ Date: _____ **15**

_____ 6. Which of the following may not be a feature of future Landsats?
      a. heat measurement
      b. radar
      c. X-ray
      d. photographs of smaller areas

_____ 7. Which will receive Landsat information in the future?
      a. Zaire
      b. China
      c. Argentina
      d. Germany

_____ 8. Which is not a natural disaster?
      a. a large forest fire
      b. crops growing
      c. melting ice near the North and South Poles
      d. lines in the earth where earthquakes might happen

_____ 9. One advantage of Landsat is
      a. it can produce more accurate maps than have been possible before.
      b. it can save time and money in the search for oil.
      c. it can predict the size of food crops.
      d. all the above.

_____ 10. Reading Landsat photos requires special training because
      a. the United States does not give out Landsat information.
      b. only patches of color can be seen.
      c. the system has many problems to be solved.
      d. only colorblind people can do it because the pictures are in false colors.

FINAL LISTENING ASSIGNMENT: NOTE-TAKING

Directions: *Read these questions before you listen to the lecture for the third time. While you are listening, write the answers.*

1. What are Landsats?

2. How do Landsats work?

3. If Landsat photos don't show things as small as people or cars, how can they show how population is growing?

Landsat System Update

Although there have been some problems with the Landsat system, in many ways the satellites have worked even better and longer than scientists had expected.

Landsats 1 and 2 were sent into space in 1972 and 1975. They were expected to work for about two years each, but they surprised scientists by sending back information for more than five and a half years. During that unusually long time, there were some changes in their performance.

The first change involved the Landsats' tape-recording *capabilities*. Originally each Landsat had two tape recorders which *enabled* them to take pictures of areas where there are no ground stations. The tape recorders held the pictures until the Landsat passed near a ground station. The pictures were then sent down. By the end of 1977, only one tape recorder of the four was working, and it was working only part of the time. During the times it was not working, Landsat pictures could only be sent to earth when the satellite was within *range* of a ground station.

Second, the orbit of Landsat 1 changed. At the time Landsat 2 was *launched* in 1975, it was placed so that together the two Landsats would pass over the same spot on earth every nine days. But by the time Landsat 1 had been in orbit four to five years, its orbit had begun to change due to the pull of earth's gravity. Therefore, it was necessary to fire Landsat 1 rockets for a very short time to correct its orbit. With the new orbit, the two satellites no longer followed each other every nine days. Instead, Landsat 1 followed Landsat 2 six days behind it, and Landsat 2 followed Landsat 1 twelve days behind it.

A third change concerned the *complex* machine that measured colors in order to send pictures back to earth. The machine was intended to measure four colors, but the part of the machine that *indicated* the color green in Landsat 1 stopped working, and for a time the spacecraft continued to operate with three color bands. Landsat 1 was finally shut down in early 1978 after five and a half years of operation.

Landsat 3 was launched to take the place of Landsat 1. Landsat 3 had the same uses as Landsat 1, and in addition, it was equipped with an *infrared* system to measure heat. This system failed after about two months. Landsat 4 is scheduled to be launched in 1981. It may also be equipped to measure heat if scientists can solve the

Figure 2. Seasat satellite.

Photograph courtesy of National Aeronautics and Space Administration.

problems that they had with Landsat 3. Landsat 5 (Stereosat) will be next. It will provide *three-dimensional* pictures of geological formations to help gas and oil companies find new sources of oil.

Seasat A was another satellite added to the Landsat system (see Figure 2). It was specifically created to gather information about the seas. *Microwave* instruments on the spacecraft were so accurate that they were supposed to be able to measure the height of the waves in the ocean to within 20 cm. (7.8 in.). Other uses for the Seasat were to watch the weather over the seas, to *forecast* storms and *floods*, and to provide information on *surface* temperatures, *currents*, and ice. Unfortunately, after operating for only 105 days, Seasat failed in October 1978 because of a loss of power.

The Landsat satellite system has sent back more data than has ever been completely and fully used. The system will continue to change. New ideas will be tried; some will fail and some will succeed. People who are interested in Landsats may read and listen for news about the Landsats in the future. At this point, nobody knows whether the program will be supported and expanded by the government, whether data will be sent to many other countries, and how data will be more fully used.

---

capability   capacity; ability

enable   make something possible

range   the area of activity

launch   to send; to set in motion

complex   consisting of interconnected parts

indicate   show

infrared   wavelengths greater than light, but shorter than microwaves

three-dimensional   showing length, width, and height

microwave   an electromagnetic radiation with a wavelength of from 1 millimeter to 1 meter

forecast   to predict, to tell what is going to happen in the future

flood   an overflowing of water onto land that is normally dry

surface   on the top

current   the steady, smooth onward movement of flowing water

Comprehension Questions

1. In what ways have Landsat satellites performed even better than they were supposed to?

2. What was the purpose of the tape recorders aboard the Landsats? How did Landsats operate differently without them?

3. Why was it necessary to change the orbit of Landsat 1?

4. What was the Landsats' new schedule?

5. Why do you think it was necessary for Landsats 1 and 2 to follow the same route?

6. What was the purpose of the Seasat A satellite?

7. Give an example to show that the Seasat A instruments were supposed to be very accurate.

8. How could information from the Seasat be used?

9. How much time do you think has passed between the Landsat lecture and this reading? From what sources can you find out about future changes?

10. Do you think the results from Landsats are worth all the work and expense?

11. This supplementary reading contains a numbered listing similar to that in the lecture. Practice your skills by outlining the reading.

    I. Introduction: Unusual length of operation has caused some changes in the two satellites' performance.

       A. The first change

       _____

       _____

B. The second change

_____

_____

_____

_____

_____

C. The third change

_____

_____

_____

_____

_____

II. Additional satellites

    A. _____

    B. _____

    C. _____
    D. Seasat: Uses

        1. _____

        2. _____

        3. _____

        4. _____

III. The future of the Landsat system

_____

_____

_____

_____

LISTENING TEST: COMMUNICATIONS SATELLITES

Incomplete Outline

I. Introduction

A. Russia sent the first satellite into space in _____.

B. _____ man-made objects have been launched into

space; _____ are still in space.

C. The smallest objects weigh _____;

the largest ones weigh _____.

II. One very useful kind of working satellite is the communica-

tions satellite. Communication means _____.

III. How are communications satellites used?

A. The first use is to _____.

B. Another use is to _____.

C. The third use is to _____.

    1. Examples

        a. International Olympic Games
        b.
        c.

IV. Who owns satellites?

    A. Russia
    B. The United States

    C. _____

    D. _____
    E. Canada

    F. _____

    G. _____

V. What can a country that doesn't have a communications satellite do?

    A. It can buy information from a private company called

    _____.

    B. More than _____ countries are members of this company.

True-False Questions

1.	6.
2.	7.
3.	8.
4.	9.
5.	10.

SOLAR ENERGY:
AN ENERGY
ALTERNATIVE

INTRODUCTION TO THE LECTURE

Topic: How Solar Heating of Buildings Works

The most widely used types of energy in the United States up to the present have been natural gas, oil, and coal; all three are fuels that exist in limited quantities in the earth. New energy sources which do not depend as much on the earth's resources are nuclear power and solar energy. This lecture explores the possibilities of using energy from the sun, solar energy.

Thesis: Solar Energy May Solve the Energy Problems of the Future

Because the supply of oil is very limited, we need to develop new sources of energy as quickly as possible. Solar energy may be a good solution to our energy needs.

Organizational Strategy: Generalizations and Supporting Examples and Steps in a Process

First the lecturer lists various sources of energy, describing their advantages and disadvantages. Then she explains the process for heating buildings with solar energy.

Figure 3. Solar-heated three-bedroom house.

Photograph by Patricia Wilcox Peterson.

     I. Introduction: The need for new energy sources
    II. Other sources of energy available to us
   III. The solar heating of buildings

BASIC SENTENCES

Directions: *Together the basic sentences provide a short summary of the main ideas in the lecture. Read and study these sentences before you listen to the lecture for the first time.*

1. In the United States today we are using more and more oil every day, and the future supply is very limited.

2. There are three other sources of energy available to us: coal, nuclear energy, and solar energy.

Figure 4. Solar-heated apartment building.

Figure 5. Solar-heated condominiums.

Photographs by Patricia Wilcox Peterson.

Figure 6. Diagram of the hot-air solar heating system.

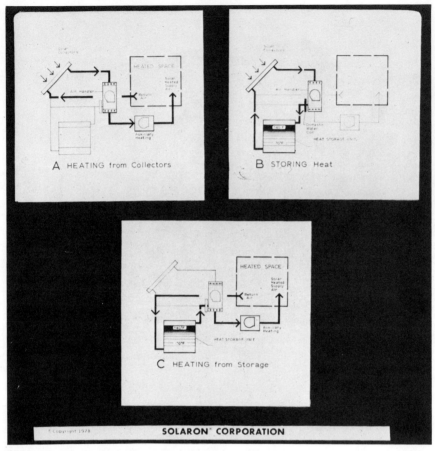

Photograph courtesy of Solaron Corporation, Denver, Colorado.

3. The federal government is spending millions of dollars to find ways to convert, or change, sunshine into economical energy.

4. There is no need to purchase fuel to operate a solar heating system because sunshine is free to everyone.

5. Once the system is installed, or put in, little or no maintenance is necessary.

6. The second advantage of solar heat is that it can be used almost anywhere.

7. In practice, the major expense involved in a solar heating system is the purchase cost of all the parts of the system and the cost of their installation.

8. An additional expense is the cost of an alternate heating system.

9. There are two main types of solar heating systems: hot-air and hot-liquid systems.

10. The parts of each system are: a collector, a storage unit, a thermostat, and an auxiliary heating unit.

11. New designs and mass production may lower the cost of solar heating systems in a few years.

ADDITIONAL VOCABULARY

Directions: *Below are some additional words that may be new to you. Look up the ones you don't know before listening to the lecture.*

estimate	mine	uranium
inadequate	switched on	

Listening Cues: Vocabulary of Numerical Order

first	third	then
second		

STUDY SKILLS

Exercise One: Classification

Below is a list of information. Organize the list into outline form.

A storage unit

Hot-air systems

A collector

An auxiliary heating unit

Hot-liquid systems

A thermostat

I. Main types of solar heating systems

    A. ——————————————

    B. ——————————————

II. Parts of each system

    A. ——————————————

    B. ——————————————

    C. ——————————————

    D. ——————————————

Solar comes from the Latin word *sol*, meaning sun.

There are problems with mining it.

Production of new nuclear power plants has slowed down because of public concern over their safety.

There are problems with developing a way to burn it without polluting the air.

The amount of solar energy falling on the continental United States is 700 times our total consumption.

There are problems with transporting it.

The government once thought we would be getting 20% of our electric-

I. Other sources of energy available to us

    A. Coal

        1. ——————————————

           ——————————————

        2. ——————————————

           ——————————————

        3. ——————————————

           ——————————————

ity from nuclear energy by the 1970s, but it produces only about 12% as of 1979.

B. Nuclear energy

1. _____

_____

2. _____

_____

C. Solar energy

1. _____

_____

2. _____

_____

Exercise Two: Classification

In order to classify ideas together correctly, you need to know which ideas are related and which are not. In the following exercise, three words or terms in each line are related and one is not. Decide what the related words have in common. Circle the one word that is not related to the others.

1. endless	(inadequate)	unlimited	infinite
2. auxiliary	practical	supplementary	alternate
3. obvious	current	modern	present
4. fuel	power	consumption	energy
5. install	produce	develop	invent
6. coal	oil	uranium	furnace
7. expense	cost	finance charge	source
8. solar	maintenance	sunshine	sol
9. run out	estimate	guess	figure

Exercise Three: Recognizing Main Topics and Subtopics

Below is a list of sentences in random order about solar energy. First, read all the sentences. Look for the best way they might be organized into an outline. Then copy each sentence on the appropriate lines in the blank outline.

The second advantage is that it can be used almost anywhere.

This is a one-time cost that can be financed over many years.

What are the advantages of solar heating for buildings?

The major disadvantage of a solar heating system is the cost of the parts of the system and the cost of their installation.

The first is that it is cheaper to operate than gas or oil.

The approximate cost to buy and install a solar system in a three-bedroom house is $7,000 to $12,000.

I. _____

    A. _____

    B. _____

II. _____

    A. _____

    B. _____

Exercise Four: Main Ideas and Supporting Details

Practice finding main ideas and supporting ideas. Notice the organization of the following material from the lecture. Find and write the main idea and supporting ideas in the outlines below.

Many experts believe that we must turn to the sun to solve our energy needs. Solar energy is clean and unlimited. It is estimated that the amount of solar energy falling on the continental United States is 700 times our total energy consumption. By the year 2000, solar technology could be supplying about 25 percent of the United States' energy needs.

Name: _____ Date: _____ **35**

I. _____ (main idea)

   _____

  A. _____ (supporting idea)

    _____

  B. _____ (supporting idea)

    _____

  C. _____ (supporting idea)

    _____

The major expense involved in a solar heating system is the purchase cost of all the parts of the system and the cost of their installation. The approximate cost to buy and put a solar heating system into a three-bedroom house at the present is $7,000 to $12,000. This is a one-time cost that can be financed over many years. This finance charge may be more expensive than heating with oil at the present prices.

I. _____ (main idea)

   _____

  A. _____ (supporting idea)

    _____

  B. _____ (supporting idea)

    _____

  C. _____ (supporting idea)

    _____

INCOMPLETE OUTLINE

Directions: *Read the outline before you listen to the lecture for the first time, so you will know what kinds of things you need to listen for. While you are listening, find the missing dates and phrases to complete the outline. Mark your paper while you listen. You have been given the answers to part III. C–2 so you can look at the diagram as you listen.*

I. Introduction: The need for new energy sources

    A. For the last _____ years, oil has been an inexpensive source of energy.

    B. Oil may be a major source of energy for only _____ more years.

II. Other sources of energy available to us

    A. Coal

        1. Advantage: We have a lot.
        2. Disadvantages: There may be problems with

        _____ it, _____ it, and developing a way to _____ it without polluting the air.

    B. Nuclear energy

        1. Advantage: We have enough uranium for a long time.

        2. Disadvantages: Public concern over the _____ of nuclear energy. The government once thought we

        would be getting _____% of our electricity

        from nuclear energy by the _____, but nuclear

        energy produced only about _____% as of 1979.

C. Solar energy (from Latin *sol*, meaning _____)

    1. Advantages

        a. It is clean and unlimited.

        b. The amount falling on the U.S. is _____ times our total energy consumption.

        c. By 2000, it could supply _____% of U.S. energy needs.

    2. Disadvantage: The cost of converting sunshine to solar energy is high.

III. The solar heating of buildings

    A. Advantages

        1. It is cheaper than gas or oil.

            a. There is no need to purchase _____.

            b. Little or no _____ is necessary.

        2. It can be used almost anywhere.

    B. Disadvantages

        1. Purchase cost

            a. The cost for a three-bedroom house is

              $_____.

            b. This is a _____ cost that can be financed over many years.

        2. Additional cost — alternative heating system

            a. Solar systems can't always provide _____% of your heat.

            b. You must have a _____, _____, or

            _____ furnace.

C. How solar heating works (hot-air and hot-liquid)

   1. Parts

      a. _____

      b. _____

      c. _____

      d. _____

   2. Hot-air system

      a. The collector catches _the sun's rays_.

      b. The sun heats _the panels_.

      c. The panels heat _the air inside_.

      d. On sunny days when heat is needed, hot air flows to

         the thermostat, into the _the building_,
         and back to the collector.

      e. On sunny days when heat is not needed, hot
         air flows to the thermostat, then into

         the storage unit.

      f. At night, the thermostat sends air from the

         storage unit into the building.

   3. Hot-liquid system

      a. It contains _____ instead of air.

      b. The storage unit is _____.

WORD RECOGNITION EXERCISE

Directions: *Fill the blanks in each word family by finding the missing parts of speech in your dictionary. Divide each word into syllables and mark the syllable that takes primary stress, as shown.*

Word Families

Noun	Verb	Adjective	Adverb
1. ———	———	pro duc′ tive	———
2. ———	de scribé	———	———
3. ———	———	es′ ti ma ted	XXXXXXX
4. ———	con vert′	———	XXXXXXX
5. ———	———	———	ec o nom′ i cal ly
6. ———	in stall′	XXXXXXX	XXXXXXX
7. ———	———	———	al′ ter nate ly
8. ———	———	stored	XXXXXXX
9. ———	———	con tained′	XXXXXXX
10. ———	———	———	bá si cal ly
11. ———	———	prac′ ti cal	———
12. prof′ it	———	———	———
13. ———	———	min′ er al	XXXXXXX
14. ———	XXXXXXX	sys tem at′ ic	———

TRUE-FALSE EXERCISE

Directions: *Read these sentences before you listen to the lecture for the second time. While you are listening, decide whether each item is true or false. Mark your paper with a T for true or an F for false while you listen.*

_____ 1. Burning coal causes pollution.

_____ 2. Many more new nuclear power plants are being built every year.

_____ 3. Solar heating systems are cheaper to operate than gas or oil systems.

_____ 4. Solar systems provide 100% of your heat.

_____ 5. Solar heat cannot be used in colder areas of the world.

_____ 6. In a collector, the sun heats the black panels, which heat the air inside.

_____ 7. The auxiliary heating unit is a container of small, round rocks.

_____ 8. On cloudy days, hot air from the collector flows to the thermostat, through the building's heating system, and out into the house.

_____ 9. Hot-liquid systems operate in basically the same way as hot-air systems except that they contain liquid instead of air.

_____ 10. You can buy a solar heating system in most large stores.

TOPICS FOR DISCUSSION AND WRITING

1. Many other products besides fuel can be made from oil. Some examples are plastics, dyes, fertilizers, cosmetics, and synthetic fibers such as polyester. Tell or write about some possible problems, besides those that are energy-related, that may arise when the supply of oil runs out.

2. Even countries (such as Saudi Arabia) that are rich in oil are concerned about what may happen when there is no more oil left. For this reason, Saudi Arabia has given millions of dollars to help support solar energy research in the United States. What characteristics does Saudi Arabia have that would make it a good location for solar energy stations?

3. Discuss some methods of fuel conservation that would help the world's supply of oil last longer.

4. Look at the diagram of the solar heating system in this unit. Present an oral description or write about the process, telling how solar heating works

   a. on sunny days when heat is needed
   b. on sunny days when heat is not needed
   c. on cloudy days or at night when heat is needed

5. Why do you think the collector panels must cover such a large area of the roof? Will houses need to be designed in new ways to accommodate solar collectors?

6. Do you think the houses in the pictures accompanying the lecture are attractive, or do the collectors spoil the appearance of the houses? What do you think houses of the future will look like?

7. Some people think the thermostat may be the most important part of a solar heating system. Why would this be true?

MULTIPLE CHOICE EXERCISE

Directions: *Choose the one answer that best completes each sentence. Write the letter of the correct answer in the blank.*

_____ 1. Oil may not be a major source of energy after only _____ more years.
   a. 50
   b. 75
   c. 25
   d. none of the above

_____ 2. Which is *not* a problem related to coal?
   a. mining it
   b. purchasing it
   c. transporting it
   d. developing a way to burn it without polluting the air

3. Which is a problem related to nuclear energy?
   a. lack of uranium to fuel nuclear power plants
   b. converting nuclear energy to electricity
   c. the safety of nuclear energy
   d. none of the above

4. Which is *not* true about solar energy?
   a. It is clean.
   b. It is unlimited.
   c. It is cheaper than gas or oil.
   d. It can always provide enough heat for your house.

5. Solar heating is most practical in areas of the United States where
   a. there is a lot of winter sunshine.
   b. heat is necessary.
   c. fuel is expensive.
   d. all of the above.

6. The part of the solar heating system which directs the air into the house or into the storage unit is
   a. the collector.
   b. the thermostat.
   c. the auxiliary heating unit.
   d. the panels.

7. What contains metal panels coated with black paint to absorb the heat?
   a. thermostat
   b. storage unit
   c. auxiliary heating unit
   d. collector

8. On sunny days when heat is needed, the thermostat
   a. sends the hot air to a storage unit.
   b. sends the air directly into the building's heating system.
   c. sends the air through an auxiliary heating unit and then throughout the building.
   d. sends the air directly back to the collector.

9. On cloudy days or at night the thermostat takes air from the storage unit and then
   a. sends the hot air to a storage unit.

Name: _____   Date: _____   **43**

b. sends the air directly into the building's heating system.
c. sends the air through an auxiliary heating unit and then throughout the building.
d. sends the air directly back to the collector.

_____ 10. Which of the following ideas is implied but not stated in the
lecture?
a. We have not been careful about our use of energy in the past.
b. Some people think that nuclear energy is not safe.
c. The only use of solar energy is for heating buildings.
d. The federal government is not encouraging the development of
   solar energy.

FINAL LISTENING ASSIGNMENT: NOTE-TAKING

Directions: *Read these questions before you listen to the lecture for
the third time. While you are listening, write the answers.*

1. What are the problems with coal, oil, and nuclear energy?

2. Describe the characteristics of the areas in the United States
   where solar heating is most practical.

3. Using Figure 6 at the beginning of this chapter, tell how a hot-air
   solar heating system works.

ENERGY POSSIBILITIES FOR THE FUTURE

Two imaginative ideas would supply people on earth with energy from space. One idea *proposes* a solar power station that would orbit the earth and send energy back by microwaves. The other proposes a power-relay satellite. The satellite would *transmit* power from a solar or nuclear power station located in an isolated place on earth to a receiving station serving a populated area on earth.

The Orbiting Solar Power Station

This idea calls for a very large solar collector in orbit around the earth. The one shown in Figure 7 would be 7 miles or 12 kilometers long. The design in Figure 8 calls for the use of *solar cells* to collect electricity. The electricity would be sent to earth by microwaves.

Figure 7. Orbiting solar collector.

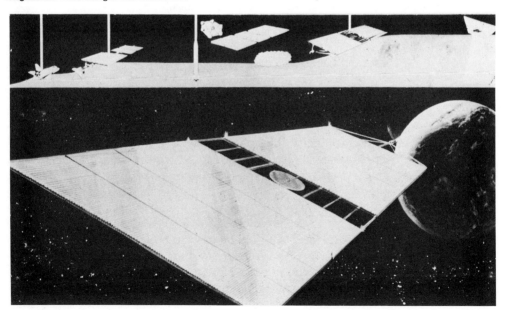

Photograph courtesy of National Aeronautics and Space Administration.

Figure 8. Solar power system.

Photograph courtesy of National Aeronautics and Space Administration.

The microwaves would be collected by a very large receiving *antenna* and converted back to electricity.

An orbiting solar power station has several advantages. There are no clouds to block the sunlight from a solar receiver high in space. The sun is always shining in space; there are no day-and-night cycles. One orbiting station of 15 million *kilowatts* could supply all the electric needs of a city the size of New York City in the year 2000.

There are several disadvantages to an orbiting solar power system. First, the extremely large solar collector would have to be carried into space piece by piece in rockets and then put together in space by astronauts. This would be very expensive and difficult; some new technological advances will be necessary before this can be done. Second, the solar cells that will be used to collect the solar energy are very expensive at present. Finally, further experiments will be necessary to determine whether it will be possible or even safe to send the electricity back to earth by microwaves. There are still some important problems to be solved, but the designers of outer-space solar power stations think they can be ready for use within twenty years.

The Power-Relay Satellite

This plan calls for a large solar or nuclear power station to operate in an isolated place on earth, perhaps in the desert. A power-relay satellite would be placed in orbit to relay the energy to cities in much the same way that a communications satellite relays TV and telephone calls now. The largest and heaviest parts of the system would stay on the ground; this would reduce the cost and difficulty. Because this idea also calls for relaying the energy by microwave, much more experimentation needs to be done before this idea can become a reality.

---

propose suggest

transmit send

solar cell a device, about the size of a large button, made of silicon crystal. As light strikes the cell, it causes positive and negative charges and starts an electric current flowing.

antenna metallic device for sending or receiving electromagnetic waves

kilowatt measurement of electricity

Comprehension Questions

1. How large a collector is proposed for an orbiting solar power station?

2. How would electricity be collected?

3. How would it be sent back to earth?

4. What are the advantages of an orbiting solar power station? What are the disadvantages?

5. Describe how a power-relay satellite will work.

LISTENING TEST: ENERGY FROM THE SEA

Incomplete Outline

I. The sea is a natural solar collector.

    A. _____% of the earth near the equator is covered by water.

    B. This area receives _____ of the total solar energy falling on the earth.

II. Scientists have experimented with large energy farms in the sea.

    A. Kelp is _____.

        1. It can grow _____ feet in one day.

        2. Almost _____% of the energy in kelp can be used for fuel.

    B. Kelp can be used to make

        1. Methane gas and methyl alcohol which are _____

_____ .

    2. Steam to produce _____ .

III. There are three advantages to having energy farms in the sea.

    A. First, it does not use _____ .

    B. Second, there is no need to worry about _____ .

    C. Third, these farms can be placed _____

_____ .

IV. Dr. Richard Bogan of the Energy Research and Development Administration (ERDA) has said that

    A. A farm could be established in _____ .

    B. This farm would only take _____ % of this space.

    C. We could grow enough kelp to supply energy for _____

_____ .

True-False Questions

1.	6.
2.	7.
3.	8.
4.	9.
5.	10.

Barter:
An Old Idea
with New Power

INTRODUCTION TO THE LECTURE

Topic: Trade With and Without Money

Trade has been occurring ever since human beings began to interrelate; the desire to exchange things is the center of any market system. Trade can be conducted with money as the medium of exchange, as is commonly done in the modern world. Alternatively, goods can be bartered for other goods. Finally, some combination of these two systems may be used.

Thesis: Barter Has a Place in the Modern World

Bartering was a form of trade used before money was invented; recently, because of inflation and the differences between types of currency around the world, bartering has become an important form of trade again.

Organizational Strategy: Definition of Terms

This lecture is a general introduction to the subjects of trade, money, and barter. One of the speaker's main goals is to provide definitions of the topics.

I. Trading in the market system

   A. Trading without money
   B. The evolution to a monetized society
   C. Trading with money

II. Barter in the modern world

   A. Reasons for barter

      1. Types of currency
      2. Inflation

   B. Examples

Figure 9(a). Barter system: Seashells being bartered for spices.

Figure 9(b). Barter and money systems operating together.

Drawings by Jans B. Wagner, EMC Graphics Dep't., University of Colorado.

BASIC SENTENCES

Directions: *Together the basic sentences provide a short summary of the main ideas in the lecture. Read and study these sentences before you listen to the lecture for the first time.*

1. The desire to exchange things is the center of any market system, regardless of whether it is a centrally planned market system or a free market system.

2. Trade has been occurring ever since early human beings began to interrelate.

3. By bartering trade can be conducted without money to pay for goods.

4. Bartering is the process by which trade takes place through the exchange of goods.

5. As trade became more common, it was necessary to develop or invent a more convenient method of payment.

6. Whereas seashells and spices had no specified value, this new money had a stated value.

7. The money — or currency, as money is referred to — of some countries is more valuable than that of other countries.

8. We refer to the more valuable currency as hard currency, while we term the less valuable money soft currency.

9. Without hard currency, it is difficult to make purchases in the international marketplace.

10. Inflation refers to an abnormally rapid increase in prices; therefore, inflation erodes the purchasing power of the already scarce hard currency held by some nations.

11. It is obvious that the conventional method of payment in hard currency must be supplemented by other types of payment such as bartering.

12. It is difficult to give examples of barter deals because in most cases, the terms of the contract are not disclosed.

13. Finding a market for bartered goods can be a problem.

14. It is unlikely that the world will revert to a totally barter-oriented existence.

15. Until the economic disorder that is present in today's world is remedied, bartering will probably become increasingly important as an exchange medium.

ADDITIONAL VOCABULARY

Directions: *Below are some additional words that may be new to you. Look up the ones you don't know before listening to the lecture.*

apricots	frequency	profit
competitor	insignificant	propensity
consumer	interim	significant
evolution	medium	syrup
extent	monetize	transaction
	precise	vodka

Listening Cues: Vocabulary of Contrast, Additional Information, and Cause and Effect

These words show contrast:

although	whereas	while
instead	however	

> It is true that most trade today takes place with money as the exchange medium. *However,* due to recent economic developments, the world is once again conducting trade by bartering.

The word *however* signals that the information following it will contrast with the sentence before.

These words show additional information:

furthermore	in fact	moreover

> Most countries that possess soft currency find it quite difficult to obtain hard currency; *moreover,* they face the problem of inflation.

The word *moreover* signals that the next sentence will contain information that can be added to the one before.

These words show cause and effect:

consequently	therefore	as a result of

> It was necessary to develop a more convenient method of payment. *Consequently,* a new form of exchange medium, money, was introduced into society.

The word *consequently* signals that the information following it is the result of the information in the sentence before.

Exercise One: Writing Definitions

When you are listening to a lecture, it is often necessary to be able to recognize and write good definitions. Particularly in introductory lectures, there will be a large number of new terms for you to learn. There is a general form that you can use to make English definitions easier for you to write.

The first rule is that you should define a word with a word that is the same part of speech. That is, define nouns with nouns, verbs with verbs, adjectives with adjectives, and so on. Because the specialized vocabulary of most academic fields is a naming process, most new terms will be nouns. Here is a formula for defining nouns: Place the word in a general familiar category first, and then tell more about its distinguishing features.

Noun	General Category	Distinguishing Features
A tiger is	a member of the wild cat family	that has striped fur.
A vulture is	a bird	that eats the flesh of dead animals.
A democracy is	a system of government	in which the people hold the power either directly or through elected representatives.

Practice: Make definitions for the following nouns:

A tree is _____   _____

_____   _____

Homework is _____   _____

_____   _____

A chair is _____   _____

_____   _____

Name: _____   Date: _____   **55**

A pencil is   _____   _____

_____   _____

Happiness is   _____   _____

_____   _____

Exercise Two: Recognizing the Main Idea

One of the most important skills you can develop as you listen to lectures is to be able to recognize the main idea the speaker is discussing. You have already learned that very often the speaker will help you with listening cues (rhetorical questions, numbers, and certain other words). These cues point out the main ideas and help you recognize transitions from one part of the lecture to the next. Often a well-organized speaker will announce his or her topic clearly with phrases such as these:

"My next point is . . ."
"Let's move on to another matter . . ."
"Another problem to be discussed . . ."
"A related area would be . . ."

Some professors are better organized than others, of course, and there will be times when your teacher doesn't seem to give you much help! However, it is your job to decide what she or he is talking about. You must be able to identify the main topic in order to take good notes.

Directions: *Your teacher will read these paragraphs to you. Cover the paragraph as he or she reads. Then decide what topic heading you would use to describe the main idea of each. Write the topic heading about each paragraph. The first example is done for you.*

1. *Trading without money (barter)*

How was trade conducted without money to pay for goods? The answer is by bartering. Bartering is the process by which trade takes place by the exchange of goods. Money is not used as payment. Instead, one good is traded for another good.

2. _____

Of course, the evolution from a total barter society to one that was totally monetized did not occur overnight. In fact, today there are still societies that are not monetized, although they account for an insignificant amount of world trade. In the interim between a barter world and a monetized world, both systems operated together.

3. _____

As I stated earlier, money has a specific value; but due to certain conditions, the money — or currency, as money is referred to — of some countries is more valuable than that of other countries. We refer to the more valuable currency as hard currency, while we term the less valuable money soft currency.

4. _____

It is difficult to give examples of barter deals because in most cases the terms of the contract are not disclosed. In some cases, we don't hear about barter transactions simply because they work so well. If one company has arranged a profitable exchange, it will be very quiet about it so that its competitors will not come in and try to make a better deal.

Exercise Three: Rephrasing Sentences for Note-Taking

Taking good notes requires you to be able to do two things very quickly: First, you must recognize main topics; second, you must be able to write down as many details and supporting examples as you can hear and understand. In other words, your hand must work as quickly as your ear.

Most students do not have special training in transcribing, or copying, speech. You don't need a course in secretarial skills or shorthand in order to do a good job taking notes. But you do need to practice a few simple techniques to help you to be thorough in your note-taking. You should use abbreviations. We will study that technique more in the next lesson. You should also learn how to write only the most important words from each sentence, and ignore the rest.

When you send a telegram to somebody, you must pay by the word; and for many people, money is limited. That is why we send very short telegrams which include only the most important words. For example, compare these two messages:

1. "I will be arriving tomorrow, Monday, April 15, on TWA flight number 222, at JFK airport."
2. "Arrive 15th TWA 222 JFK"

Which message would be more expensive?

When you take notes, you have a similar problem. In this case it is not money, but time, that is limited. Therefore, it is a good idea to practice listening for only the most important sentences in a section of speech, and only the most important words in those sentences.

Directions: *Listen to the following sentences as your teacher reads them. You may be able to tell which words are most important by the stress and volume of a person's voice. Key words are stressed and spoken more loudly. Write the words you think are most important in the space below each sentence. The first example is done for you.*

1. Bartering is the process by which trade takes place through the exchange of goods.

   barter = trading goods for goods

2. Whereas seashells and spices had no stated value, this new money had a stated value.

   _____

3. We refer to the more valuable currency as hard currency, while we term the less valuable money soft currency.

   _____

4. Inflation refers to an abnormally rapid increase in prices.

   _____

5. Although there are no precise figures available, it is widely known that a significant amount of trade conducted between Eastern European communist countries and the rest of the world is done by means of barter.

   _____

6. Not only is the following illustration a good example of bartering it also reveals, to a small degree, consumer preferences in beverages in the USSR and the United States.

_____

7. It seems that Pepsi Cola was the first company to introduce cola into Russia, much to the disappointment of Coca-Cola.

_____

INCOMPLETE OUTLINE

Directions: *Some lectures you will hear at the university will not fit easily into the outline form you have learned. In particular, this is true of a lecture in which the relationships between ideas are not as important as the individual terms that are discussed. "Barter—An Old Idea with New Power" is an example of this type of lecture. It is important that you be able to understand and write down the definitions of several important terms. As you listen to the lecture, use what you have learned about writing definitions to complete this outline. The terms* trading, evolution, hard currency, soft currency, *and* inflation *are all nouns. Put a definition of each of those terms where they appear in the outline.*

    I. Trading and the market system

        A. Trading without money (barter)

        _____

        _____

        B. The evolution to a monetized society

        _____

        _____

C. Trading with money

_____

_____

II. Barter in the modern world

A. Reasons for barter

1. Types of currency

a. Hard _____

b. Soft _____

2. Inflation _____

_____

B. Examples

1. Countries with no precise figures available

a. _____

b. _____

c. _____

d. _____

2. Reasons why it is difficult to give examples

a. _____

b. _____

3. Examples with public attention

a. _____

b. _____

WORD RECOGNITION EXERCISE

Directions: *Fill the blanks in each word family by finding the missing parts of speech in your dictionary. Divide each word into syllables and mark the syllable that takes the primary stress, as shown.*

Word Families

Noun	Verb	Adjective	Adverb
1. pref′er ence	————	————	————
2. ————	————	rel′a tive	————
3. ————	de pend′	————	————
4. ————	————	spe cif′ic spé cif ied	————
5. ————	val′ue	————	XXXXXXX
6. ————	————	mon′e tized	XXXXXXX
7. ab nor mal′i ty	XXXXXXX	————	————
8. ————	e rodé′	XXXXXXX	XXXXXXX
9. ————	————	sig nif′i cant	————
10. ————	————	————	fré quent ly
11. oc cur′rence	————	XXXXXXX	XXXXXXX
12. ————	————	com par′a tive	————
13. ————	————	————	in ven′tive ly
14. ————	XXXXXXX	scarce	————
15. dis cló sure	————	————	XXXXXXX

MAKING NEW WORDS

The prefix *inter* means *between*. You have learned the word *interim*, which means a period of time *between* two other time periods or events.

Below are several words you already know. Make new words by adding the prefix *inter*. Tell what each new word means and use it in a sentence. The first example is done for you.

dependence   *interdependence*   dependence between two people, groups of people, or things.

People who barter show their interdependence by trading together.

relate _____   _____

_____

national _____   _____

_____

change _____   _____

_____

state _____   _____

_____

racial _____   _____

_____

action _____   _____

_____

mix   _____   _____

_____

marriage   _____   _____

_____

tribal   _____   _____

_____

TRUE-FALSE EXERCISE

Directions: *Read these sentences before you listen to the lecture for the second time. While you are listening, decide whether each item is true or false. Mark your paper with a T for true or an F for false while you listen.*

_____   1. Adam Smith said that trade occurs only in a free-market system.

_____   2. Barter is relatively new when it is seen in relation to the length of time trade has been conducted.

_____   3. Money is convenient to use because it has a specific value.

_____   4. All societies are monetized today.

_____   5. There is a high demand for soft currency.

_____   6. Inflation hurts countries with soft currency.

_____   7. Eastern European countries have disclosed their barter deals.

_____   8. Americans traded one gallon of Pepsi-Cola for one gallon of Russian vodka.

_____ 9. The world may someday again conduct trade only by bartering.

_____ 10. Bartering is becoming more frequent because of the poor condition of the world economy.

TOPICS FOR DISCUSSION AND WRITING

1. The lecturer says that "the desire to exchange things is the center of any market system regardless of whether it is a *centrally planned market system* or a *free market system*." In economics, the American market system is usually described as a free-market system, since the laws of supply and demand determine the price and production of most things. The Russian market system is described as centrally planned, since the government determines the price and production of most things.
   Give an example from the lecture that shows that both market systems depend on trade.

2. Even in monetized societies, some groups of people may occasionally trade goods for goods. Below are a few examples. Can you think of things that these people might trade with one another?

   Two children playing with their toys

   Two women who wear the same size clothes

   Two sets of parents who want to go out in the evenings, but who don't want to pay a babysitter to take care of their children

   Two artists or craftsmen who admire each other's work

   Can you think of more examples of trading that occurs without money?

3. In the past, many different exchange media were used before money was invented: spices, shells, grain, cattle. As people began to travel greater distances through many kinds of bad weather, money became more common and replaced the other exchange media. What advantages does money have that make it easier to use than spices, shells, grain, or cattle?

4. Can you name some countries with hard currency? With soft currency?

5. Do you know what has happened to the value of your country's currency in the last five years? Tell how inflation has affected your country, and give some examples.

6. Which of these factors would make the value of a nation's cur-

rency go down in international trade? Which factors would cause the value to increase?

The discovery of oil

Inflation in the country

A pattern of importing (bringing in) more goods than the country exports (sells)

A pattern of exporting more goods than the country imports

Labor union strikes

Very highly developed science and technology

Civil war

Many years of peace

7. Describe your country's place in international trade. Tell what things you must import from other countries. Also tell which things you export to other countries.

MULTIPLE CHOICE EXERCISE

Directions: *Choose the one answer that best completes each sentence. Write the letter of the correct answer in the blank.*

_____ 1. Trade is
   a. the same as barter.
   b. a system of exchanging goods for other goods.
   c. a system of exchanging things with money.
   d. a system of exchange with or without money.

_____ 2. In modern times, we find that
   a. almost all societies are monetized.
   b. barter only occurs between less developed nations.
   c. some trade still occurs through barter.
   d. a and c.

_____ 3. The lecturer says that one pound of spices
   a. has the value of 10 seashells.
   b. has the value of 100 sheashells.
   c. has no specified value.
   d. none of the above.

Name: _____ Date: _____

4. One reason trade became more common is that
   a. money was invented.
   b. people became more dependent on one another.
   c. inflation caused prices to rise.
   d. none of the above.

5. Some countries have problems in international trade because
   a. their currency is more valuable than that of other countries.
   b. they possess soft currency.
   c. they possess hard currency.
   d. a and c.

6. Last year a bottle of orange juice cost $.40. This year the price is $.65. This increase in price is an example of
   a. inflation.
   b. a centrally planned market system.
   c. a free market system.
   d. an increase in purchasing power.

7. Barter may become more important in the modern world because
   a. inflation erodes the purchasing power of all currency.
   b. without hard currency, it is difficult to make purchases in the international marketplace.
   c. barter transactions can work well.
   d. all the above.

8. In one barter deal between the USSR and the United States
   a. the Americans traded Pepsi-Cola for vodka.
   b. the Russians traded Pepsi-Cola for apricots.
   c. the Russians traded autos for vodka.
   d. the Americans traded vodka for Pepsi-Cola.

9. In one example, there were problems in finding a market for the bartered goods because
   a. the Russians became bored with vodka.
   b. the Americans became bored with apricots.
   c. the Western Europeans became bored with apricots.
   d. the Eastern Europeans became bored with Pepsi-Cola.

10. The lecturer implies, but does not state, that
    a. bartering will probably become increasingly important as an exchange medium.

b. people all over the world are similar because they have a desire
      to trade.
   c. money is relatively new when compared to the length of time
      trade has been conducted.
   d. money has a specified value.

FINAL LISTENING ASSIGNMENT: NOTE-TAKING

   Directions: *Read these questions before you listen to the lecture for
   the third time. While you are listening, write the answers. You may
   use abbreviations if you want to.*

   1. How has trade changed over the years?

   2. What are the advantages of money?

   3. Why is hard currency more useful in world trade?

   4. Why do both developed countries and developing countries use
      barter?

Barter in the Anasazi Market System

Trade has been occurring ever since early human beings began to interrelate. Before the invention of money as an exchange medium, trade already existed. Exchanges were made between individuals, between families, between villages, and between *tribes.* People bartered one kind of good, which was plentiful, for another kind of good, which was scarce. This kind of trade worked on principles of supply, demand, surplus, scarcity, and relative value, just as trade takes place in the modern marketplace today.

There are examples of early barter systems in almost every country of the world. The Anasazi Indians, an early Pueblo tribe of southwestern Colorado, provide an interesting case study. Archeologists, scientists who study the physical *remains* of a culture, have found enough *evidence* to be able to describe the Anasazi barter system around the year 1200. The Anasazi were primarily an agricultural people. They did not wander over the country as other tribes of Indians did, but stayed in one place near their farms. They lived far from the ocean. Yet in their houses and buried with them in their graves, archeologists have found many lovely seashells (see Figure 10). How did the Anasazi happen to have seashells? The answer is that they obtained them and many other things through barter.

Trading between tribes was based on a system of surplus and scarcity. Each tribe occupied a fairly large area, and its culture had developed to take advantage of the resources of that area. In the Mesa Verde area, the place where the Anasazi lived, farming was profitable and hunting was good. There were more than enough *deer* for meat. The Indians used the deerskins to make a soft white leather. They became very skilled at making stone knives for scraping the meat off the deerskins. Usually the Anasazi had more deerskins and more stone knives than they needed; that is, they had a surplus. Consequently, they had enough for trading with other tribes.

A surplus has very little value, however, if nobody wants it. There must be a need, or a demand, for goods before they can be traded. Fortunately for the Anasazi, there was a great demand for their deerskins and their knives. In fact, the southern Indians could obtain deerskins and the special deer knives only by bartering with the Anasazi. Deer were in surplus in the Mesa Verde area, but they were scarce in the southern climates. Therefore, a system of supply and demand and barter was created.

Certain things were scarce in Mesa Verde, as well. There was no

Figure 10. Objects used in the Anasazi barter system.

Shells

Photographs by Patricia Wilcox Peterson and Stuart Wier, courtesy of Mesa Verde National Park Museum.

salt. Valuable stones, which the Indians needed for their beautiful *jewelry*, had to be found elsewhere. And of course, seashells for jewelry had to come from far away. Most of these goods could be found to the south. A salt lake 200 miles south of Mesa Verde provided the salt the Indians needed; the people of that area traded it for the Anasazi's knives and deerskins. The Anasazi had to travel 200 miles southeast to obtain precious stones. Seashells were the most valuable items because they came all the way from the Pacific Ocean. As they passed from tribe to tribe, they became more and more valuable. By the time they reached Mesa Verde, seashells were very much in demand. As a result of all this trading, seashells had a high relative value, in relation to deerskins and knives.

Because of their bartering, the Anasazi enjoyed a healthy economy. Furthermore, trading brought various social and cultural benefits. Indians visiting Mesa Verde from other tribes brought news from faraway places, and they also spread ideas and new ways of living. One culture borrowed an idea from another, and the second culture improved. Archeologists think that many inventions were spread through the world this way — the *bow and arrow*, houses, *pottery*, and many other things. Therefore trade, and its earliest form, barter, have been civilizing influences all through the history of humanity.

---

tribe   a group of people, usually related to one another by family ties

remains   objects that are left after a period of time

evidence   signs, remaining objects

deer   mammals with hoofs; the males have antlers on their heads

jewelry   objects to wear around the neck, fingers, or arms for decoration; may be made of metal, shells, or precious stones

bow and arrow   a type of weapon

pottery   containers shaped from moist clay and hardened by heat

Comprehension Questions

1. How long have people been trading?

2. What do archeologists do?

3. How did the Anasazi happen to have seashells?

4. What did the Anasazi have a surplus of?

5. What was scarce in Mesa Verde, where the Anasazi lived?

6. What social and cultural benefits did the Anasazi get from bartering?

7. How did the Anasazi learn about pottery?

8. Reread the last line of the reading selection. Restate this idea in your own words and give examples.

9. Write a definition for the following terms according to the information in the reading:

    supply

    demand

    surplus

    scarcity

    relative value

10. Make an outline for the reading.

Incomplete Outline

Directions: *Read the outline before you listen to the lecture. While you are listening, complete the outline. Mark your paper while you listen.*

    I. In the United States, barter system still used

   II. Most formalized barter institution is swap shop

      A. Example: Mr. John Ludewig opened a swap shop in

          _____ to exchange duplicate wedding presents.

         1. Swap means _____.

         2. Duplicate means _____.

         3. Bride means _____.

      B. Procedure:

         1. The customer pays John _____ of the value in cash.

         2. The customer can use _____ of the value to purchase something in the shop.

         3. If the customer wants something that isn't in the shop

           right then, _____.

      C. Success: Within a year, the shop had many different items

         in stock; John was earning _____ a week.

   III. Many barter services rather than goods

      A. Example: Mrs. Leith supported herself and three children

         by _____.

B. Examples of Mrs. Leith's bartering

    1. Housekeeping jobs

        a.

        b.

        c.

    2. Other goods and services

        a.

        b.

        c.

        d.

        e.

        f. eggs, milk, fruit

        g.

        h.

C. Advantages of bartering for Mrs. Leith

    1.

    2.

True-False Questions

1.	6.
2.	7.
3.	8.
4.	9.
5.	10.

Your Personality
And Your Heart

INTRODUCTION TO THE LECTURE

Topic: The Relationship between Personality Type and Heart Disease

A new approach to the study of heart disease links people's personality and emotions to their physical health. This lecture states that a person's behavior patterns determine whether or not she or he will develop heart disease.

Thesis: Personality Type A Is the Primary Cause of Heart Disease

Scientists are certain that the immediate cause of heart attacks is arteriosclerosis and cholesterol buildup in the heart's arteries, but they are still looking for the cause of arteriosclerosis. The thesis of this lecture is that hardening of the arteries is caused by nervous reaction to stress, which produces dangerous physical conditions. This kind of nervous reaction is common to people with a Type A personality, and so they are the most likely victims of heart attacks. Thus, personality Type A is the primary cause of heart disease.

**Organizational Strategy: Cause and Effect,
Contrast and Comparison**

The lecturer outlines the problem of heart disease in the United States and examines its cause. Then he illustrates the differences between two personality types, Type A and Type B, by comparing two men, Adam and Bert.

    I. Introduction
   II. Cause of heart disease
 III. Contrast Type A (Adam) and Type B (Bert)
 IV. Change in behavior pattern → chance for a healthy life

Figure 11(a). Adam's view of life.

Photograph by Patricia Wilcox Peterson.

Figure 11(b). Bert's view of life.

Photograph by Patricia Wilcox Peterson.

Figure 12(a). Adam's use of time.

Photograph by Patricia Wilcox Peterson.

Figure 12(b). Bert's use of time.

Photograph by Patricia Wilcox Peterson.

Figure 13(a).   Adam's social habits.

Figure 13(b).   Bert's social habits.

Photographs by Patricia Wilcox Peterson.

Figure 14(a). Adam's lack of physical activity.

Figure 14(b). Bert's typical physical activity.

Photographs by Patricia Wilcox Peterson.

Figure 15(a). Adam's method of relaxation.

Figure 15(b). Bert's method of relaxation.

Photographs by Patricia Wilcox Peterson.

BASIC SENTENCES

Directions: *Together the basic sentences provide a short summary of the main ideas in the lecture. Read and study these sentences before you listen to the lecture for the first time.*

1. People with certain kinds of personalities are very likely to develop heart disease.

2. Arteriosclerosis, or hardening of the arteries, and cholesterol buildup in the coronary arteries are the immediate causes of heart disease.

3. Diet, cigarette smoking, inactivity, being overweight, and high blood pressure may not start coronary artery disease, but once it has begun, these traits can act as catalysts to speed up the process.

4. Type A people are excessively competitive, set themselves unrealistic goals, and force themselves to meet impossible deadlines.

5. People who are under a great deal of stress for short periods may develop high cholesterol and high blood pressure.

6. The brain's stress centers release certain hormones which speed the clotting time of the blood—and the clotting factor can be very harmful for heart disease patients.

7. Adam has a Type A personality, and will be very likely to develop heart disease by the time he is 60 years old.

8. Bert is a Type B, and research shows that he has almost no chance of developing heart disease before the age of 70.

9. Adam always seems to be fighting time, trying to do more things in a day than he previously has done.

10. Bert, on the other hand, never complains that he has too little time to accomplish the things that he considers truly important.

11. Adams has practically no release from his job and usually brings some work home with him.

12. Once work is behind Bert for the day, he devotes himself to three or four interesting hobbies.

13. Bert enjoys a degree of peace of mind and feels that he has been able to achieve a kind of balance in his life.

14. Quite often Adam feels that life is useless and pointless.

15. Some doctors and psychologists are now trying to train Type A individuals toward Type B behavior.

ADDITIONAL VOCABULARY

Directions: *Below are some additional words that may be new to you. Look up the ones you don't know before listening to the lecture.*

bacteria	lifestyle	stay in shape
compulsive	link	statistically
daydream	mechanism	sustaining
epidemic	positive correlation	tension
frustrate	predictor	theory
hostility	resent	virus

Listening Cues: Vocabulary of Contrast and Comparison

These words show differences:

conversely	on the other hand	however
but	in contrast	although
whereas		

Life for Adam has been full of tension and hostility, *whereas* for Bert, life has been much more enjoyable.

Bert, *on the other hand*, never complains that he has too little time to accomplish the things that he considers truly important.

Bert entertains himself by watching his surroundings.
In contrast, Adam is not a good observer.

Adam usually brings some work home; Bert, *however*, shows an opposite tendency.

Although his work is sometimes troublesome, Bert is able to put such problems out of his mind at home.

Some people have all these traits but never develop heart disease; *conversely*, many heart attack victims do not exhibit any of the companions to heart disease.

High blood pressure may not start coronary artery disease; *but* once it has begun, these traits can act as catalysts to speed up the process.

These words show similarities:

both	neither	like

Both are married, have grown children, are in their mid-50s, and have been very successful in their business careers.

Like many modern Americans, *neither* man is very religious.

There are many *like* Adam in the world today.

STUDY SKILLS

Note-Taking Techniques

"Your Personality and Your Heart" is a longer lecture than you have heard so far. It is also fairly technical, full of details and examples, and contains complicated cause-and-effect relationships. You will want to write down as many of the details as possible as you listen so that you can remember them later.

However, taking notes on a lecture like this can be difficult. How can you write everything down quickly when the words are so long? For many students, the vocabulary is new and quite technical. You may still be writing one sentence while the lecturer is five sentences further along. By the time you are finished writing and can listen again you are lost! You no longer understand what the lecturer is talking about. Or, like many students, you may decide that it is more important just to listen, and so you stop taking notes. But then at the end of the lecture you have already forgotten many important details.

There are two things that you can begin to do now to make sure that your listening and note-taking keep pace with the speaker's ideas. Use these techniques for every lecture you listen to, both now and in the future.

Develop Your Own System of Symbols and Abbreviations

It is not necessary to write out the entire word if you can understand your own abbreviation. This saves valuable time. There are quite a few function words that appear in almost every academic lecture. Some relationships between ideas can be expressed by easy mathematical symbols. And finally, in each specialized course of study, there are certain words that appear so often that you will want to develop your own abbreviations for them.

The symbols you use must make sense to you, but it is not necessary for anyone else to be able to understand them. Note-taking is a very individual skill. Of course, it will help if you review your notes soon after the lecture and rewrite them in good sentence form. Such a review will help place the material in your long-term memory. In addition, a clear outline will be very helpful later when you are studying for final exams.

Below are some of the abbreviations and symbols you can use to take notes on this lecture, "Your Personality and Your Heart."

A. Terms that appear in many academic lectures:

positive	pos	increase	inc
negative	neg	decrease	dec
men	♂	with	c̄
women	♀	majority	maj
for example	e.g.	Americans	Am
concerning	re	and	& or +
therefore	∴		

B. Mathematical symbols that express relationships between ideas:

$=$ is like, is equal to, is the same as
$\neq$ is unlike, is not the same as
$\rightarrow$ causes or yields
$\leftarrow$ is caused by
$>$ greater than
$<$ less than

C. Specialized words that appear often in this lecture:

personality	pers	cigarette	cig
heart disease	h d	physical	phys
arteriosclerosis	art	correlation	cor
cholesterol	chol	blood pressure	b p

Use the Space on Your Paper to Express Relationships between Ideas

This is a technique that you have already begun to use. Making an outline is one way to show which ideas are most important, which ideas are dependent on the main ideas, and which sentences are merely examples or illustrations. In an outline, the sentences that start closest to the margin on the left are the most important ideas. You have seen how much more helpful an outline is than an unorganized list of facts.

In this lecture, the lecturer uses a very common speaking technique: comparison and contrast. He wants to show us the differences between two people, Adam and Bert. There are two ways to do this.

He could give all of Adam's characteristics first, before going on to describe Bert. If he did this, we could make a very neat outline like this:

I. Contrast Adam and Bert

    A. Adam

        1. Family life
        2. Professional life
        3. View of life
        4. Use of time
        5. Social habits
        6. Physical activity
        7. Relaxation
        8. Spritual life

    B. Bert

        1. Family life
        2. Professional life
        3. View of life
        4. Use of time
        5. Social habits
        6. Physical activity
        7. Relaxation
        8. Spritual life

Some of the subtopics would show that Adam and Bert are similar; some would show their differences. We would be able to get a complete picture of Adam first, and then contrast this with a complete description of Bert.

However, this is not the way the lecturer organizes this speech. Instead, he uses the second possible method of organization: he compares Adam and Bert, characteristic by characteristic, talking first about Adam, then about Bert, then returning again to Adam. This is an effective technique to use in lectures, because people can't usually remember small details for a long time. If the lecturer speaks about Adam's view of life 10 minutes before he mentions Bert's view of life, we may have forgotten what he said by the time he reaches Bert! A point-by-point comparison of details doesn't strain our memory as much.

The standard outline form must be changed somewhat to fit this kind of organization. In the first outline, the section about Adam was at the top of the page, and the section about Bert was at the bottom. The paper was divided in half horizontally. For a point-by-point comparison, try dividing your paper in two parts vertically. The left half of the paper will be for Adam, the right half for Bert. Then you can still write neatly as the lecturer jumps back and forth between the two men.

    I. Contrast Adam   and Bert

       A. Similarities

          1. Family life: _____   _____

             _____   _____

          2. Professional life: _____   _____

             _____   _____

       B. Differences

          1. View of life:_____   _____

             _____   _____

          2. Use of time: _____   _____

             _____   _____

          3. Social habits: _____   _____

             _____   _____

          4. Physical activity:_____   _____

             _____   _____

          5. Relaxation: _____   _____

             _____   _____

          6. Spiritual life:_____   _____

             _____   _____

If you do not like this style of outlining, you can change it to the more standard form when you rewrite your notes. Like the symbols and abbreviations, it is simply an aid to help you write down as many details as possible, as quickly as you can. The final version of these lecture notes in the Appendix will show you how to rewrite the outline in standard form.

Exercise One: Recognizing the Main Idea

Directions: *Read these paragraphs from the lecture, or ask your teacher to read them to you. Then decide what topic heading you would use to describe the main idea of each. Write the topic heading above each paragraph.*

1. *Adam's use of time*

Adam always seems to be fighting time, trying to do more things in a day than he previously has done. If situations beyond his control cause delays in his schedule, he becomes angry and hostile. He resents people who are not on time or who do not move as quickly as he does. It is very important to him that he fill up every minute with some kind of productive activity.

2. _____

Bert is a natural listener. He can lose himself in conversation with friends or family. Bert has a few very close friends, and he works hard to keep his friendships strong.

3. _____

One means of contact with friends is the regular exercise that Bert gets. He plays handball and swims with a friend twice every week. Besides that, he tries to stay in shape with morning exercises. Bert enjoys the exercise that he gets for its own sake as well as for the fact that it has kept him healthy all his life.

4. _____

In general, Adam has very few hobbies. He used to enjoy collecting coins and reading, but now can never find enough time. Adam has practically no release from his job and usually brings some work home with him.

5. _____

Like many modern Americans, neither man is very religious. Both belong to a church, but the religious services are not a sustaining part of their lives. The difference in their spiritual makeup, however, is remarkable.

6. _____

    They have been very successful in their business careers. Both are hard workers and have achieved a position of financial security and responsibility in their jobs. Their professional lives are not easy for either of them.

7. _____

    Adam does not enjoy much self-confidence. He has never taken the time to think problems through carefully or to teach himself to think about other things. As a result, he is not a particularly creative problem-solver. He spends quite a lot of time in compulsive, repetitive nervous activity which only frustrates him more.

8. _____

    Heart attack victims who have tried to change their behavior after their first heart attack report that Type B behavior has given them a new sense of peace, freedom, and happiness. Not for anything would they return to their old lifestyle, which held them trapped like prisoners in an unhappy world of their own making.

Exercise Two: Rephrasing Sentences for Note-Taking

Directions: *Listen to the following sentences as your teacher reads them. Often you can tell which words are most important by the stress and volume of a person's voice. Key words are stressed and spoken more loudly. Write the words you think are most important in the space below each sentence. Feel free to use abbreviations and mathematical symbols. The first example is done for you.*

1. Thousands of people die of heart attacks every year.

    1000 s die / yr. _____

2. Heart disease is becoming so widespread that we can almost talk of an epidemic.

_____

3. But this epidemic is different from earlier epidemics of small-pox or typhus or the plague — because unlike the earlier diseases, heart attacks are not caused by a specific virus or bacteria.

_____

4. Statistically, it can be shown that all these factors also have a positive correlation to heart disease.

_____

5. But — and this is very important — not one of these traits, nor any combination of them, can be shown to be the primary cause of heart disease.

_____

6. They are not valid as predictors, for there are many people who have all these traits but never develop heart disease.

_____

7. Conversely, many heart attack victims do not exhibit any of the traits we think of as companions to heart disease.

_____

8. One study of urban Americans indicated that between 50 and 60% fall into the category of the Type A personality.

_____

9. Stress seems to be caused by our highly technical, highly rushed modern way of life.

_____

10. Research has shown a high correlation of personality Type A and coronary tragedy.

_____

INCOMPLETE OUTLINE

Directions: *Read the outline before you listen to the lecture for the first time, so you will know what kinds of things you need to listen for. While you are listening, find the missing dates and phrases to complete the outline. Use abbreviations wherever possible. Mark your paper while you listen.*

I. Introduction

    A. If stress and time pressure make you nervous

        1. _____

        2. _____

    B. Heart disease in the United States — like an epidemic

        1. _____

        2. _____

II. Cause of heart disease

    A. Immediate cause — arteriosclerosis and cholesterol buildup

        1. What _____?

        2. Why _____?

    B. Companions to heart disease   Relationship to heart disease

        1. *fat and cholesterol in diet* _____

        2. *cigarette smoking* _____

        3. *physical inactivity* _____

        4. *overweight* _____

        5. *high blood pressure* _____

C. First causes of arteriosclerosis and cholesterol buildup

    1. Personality Type A

        a. Traits: _____

        _____

        b. Where we find Type A people: _____

        _____

    2. Physical mechanism connecting brain and heart

        a. Effects of stress

            1. _____

            2. _____

            3. _____

            4. _____

        b. Research shows _____

III. Contrast Type A (Adam)   and   Type B (Bert)

_____   _____

    A. Similarities

        1. Family life: _____

        _____

        2. Professional life: _____

        _____

        _____

B. Differences

   1. View of life: _____   _____

      _____   _____

   2. Use of time: _____   _____

      _____   _____

   3. Social habits: _____   _____

      _____   _____

   4. Physical activity: _____   _____

      _____   _____

   5. Relaxation: _____   _____

      _____   _____

      _____   _____

   6. Spiritual life: _____   _____

      _____   _____

      _____   _____

IV. Change in behavior pattern → chance for a healthy life
    (Value of training Type A individuals in Type B behavior)

   A. _____

   B. _____

WORD RECOGNITION EXERCISE

Directions: *Fill the blanks in each word family by finding the missing parts of speech in your dictionary. Divide each word into syllables and mark the syllable that takes primary stress, as shown.*

Word Families

Noun	Verb	Adjective	Adverb
1. —————	thé o rize	—————	—————
2. —————	XXXXXXX	—————	sta tis' ti cal ly
3. —————	—————	caus' al	—————
4. ten' sion	—————	—————	—————
5. —————	—————	re sent' ful	—————
6. ac tiv' i ty	—————	—————	—————
7. —————	—————	cor rel' a tive	XXXXXXX
8. —————	val' i date	—————	—————
9. —————	—————	pre dict' a ble	—————
10. —————	XXXXXXX	—————	anx' ious ly
11. —————	ex ceed'	—————	—————
12. —————	com peté'	—————	—————
13. —————	—————	re spon' sive	—————
14. suc cess'	—————	—————	—————
15. —————	—————	—————	con' fi dent ly

Name: ————————— Date: —————————

TRUE-FALSE EXERCISE

Directions: *Read these sentences before you listen to the lecture for the second time. While you are listening, decide whether each item is true or false. Mark your paper with a T for true or an F for false while you listen.*

_____ 1. We do not really know what causes heart disease.

_____ 2. Many people with heart disease have high blood cholesterol, are overweight, smoke, or get little exercise.

_____ 3. Many people who have high cholesterol never develop heart disease.

_____ 4. Many heart disease patients have Type A personalities.

_____ 5. Rich people have Type A personalities, but poor people do not.

_____ 6. As stress has increased in modern society, the rate of heart disease has also increased greatly.

_____ 7. When people live constantly under stress, their brain centers release harmful chemicals into their bodies.

_____ 8. Bert has not been successful in his job because he doesn't work hard.

_____ 9. Bert enjoys life more than Adam does.

_____ 10. Adam tries to fill up every minute with some kind of productive activity.

_____ 11. Adam is very interested in other people.

_____ 12. Bert enjoys exercise, and it keeps him healthy.

_____ 13. Bert's use of his leisure time helps him find creative solutions to his work problems.

_____ 14. Adam is a careful, creative thinker.

_____ 15. It is possible to change one's behavior pattern.

TOPICS FOR DISCUSSION AND WRITING

1. The lecturer says that in modern society, heart disease is striking more and more younger people. How is it possible for a change in a country's culture to produce changes in the health of the people? (You might consider these factors in your answer: technology, urbanization, education, a better standard of living, pollution.)

2. Traditionally the Japanese diet has been very low in cholesterol, and the Japanese people have had a low rate of heart disease. In more recent times, foods like rice, fish, and vegetables have been replaced with bread and beef. What medical problems might you expect as a result? Can you give similar examples from your own country?

3. The lecturer makes a distinction between the words *correlation* and *cause.* He says that blood cholesterol has a high correlation with heart disease, but that blood cholesterol is not the primary cause of heart disease. In other words, two conditions may often be found together in the same person (and we say they are positively correlated) but one is not the cause of the other.

    Below are pairs of conditions or events. Tell what type of relationship exists between paired items. Are they positively correlated, negatively correlated, or does one cause the other?

A	B	Relationship
overeating	being overweight	*A causes B*
poverty	being overweight	_____
a high standard of living	being overweight	_____
cold weather	common cold	_____
good diet	common cold	_____

cold virus	common cold	_____
cigarette smoking	nervous tension	_____
cigarette smoking	lung cancer	_____
cigarette smoking	heart disease	_____

4. Many people have a combination of Type A and Type B traits, although usually one personality type is predominant. Tell how you would classify yourself, and analyze some of your behavior patterns as Type A or Type B. (You may find that some of your classmates have a very different idea about you than you have of yourself!)

5. Often people misunderstand the theory behind this lecture; they mistakenly think that Type B people are lazy, stupid, and unsuccessful. One man has said, "Of course, I dislike my Type A behavior. I don't enjoy rushing around and working so hard. But a little tension is the price I must pay for my success. I have earned many honors in my life, and I'm not willing to give them up just to be able to sit around daydreaming. Hard work is part of the American way!" Do you agree or disagree with this man? Why?

6. In your opinion, how conclusive is the evidence that supports the theory in the lecture? Is the idea that personality determines heart disease an unproven theory, a well-supported theory, or a proven fact?

7. Have you noticed any cultural differences between other countries and the United States in the way that people use time and think about time? Explain and give examples.

MULTIPLE CHOICE EXERCISE

Directions: *Choose the one answer that best completes each sentence. Write the letter of the correct answer in the blank.*

_____ 1. Personality Type A is common to
    a. 30% of all Americans.
    b. 50% of all men.
    c. the majority of urban Americans.
    d. none of the above.

2. Heart disease
   a. has increased with urbanization.
   b. has decreased with urbanization.
   c. has no correlation with urbanization.
   d. none of the above.

3. Which of the following have a positive correlation to heart disease?
   a. fat, cholesterol, and being overweight
   b. cigarette smoking and high blood pressure
   c. a and b
   b. none of the above

4. If you are fat, have high blood cholesterol and high blood pressure, smoke a lot, and exercise little
   a. you may never develop heart disease.
   b. you will certainly develop heart disease.
   c. you already have heart disease.
   d. none of the above.

5. If you are thin, have low blood cholesterol and low blood pressure, do not smoke, and exercise regularly
   a. you will never develop heart disease.
   b. you will certainly develop heart disease.
   c. you may develop heart disease anyway.
   d. none of the above.

6. If two conditions have a positive correlation,
   a. the first causes the second.
   b. the second causes the first.
   c. the two often occur together.
   d. you should avoid them both.

7. Your reaction to stressful situations
   a. has physical effects.
   b. determines your personality type.
   c. can be changed with practice.
   d. all the above.

8. Type A people
   a. are competitive and hostile.
   b. enjoy life because they are usually successful.
   c. are better educated than Type B people.
   d. never look at their watches.

9. Type B people
   a. are competitive and hostile.
   b. are not respected because they have daydreams.
   c. are usually interested in other people.
   d. spend a lot of time in compulsive, repetitive nervous activity that frustrates them more.

10. Which of the statements below best reflects the lecturer's point of view?
    a. We do not really know what causes heart disease, but some combination of factors is likely.
    b. A high-cholesterol diet is the primary cause of coronary artery disease.
    c. It has been positively proven that Type A behavior is the primary cause of heart disease.
    d. Healthy people never become anxious and hostile.

FINAL LISTENING ASSIGNMENT: NOTE-TAKING

Directions: *Read these questions before you listen to the lecture for the third time. While you are listening, write the answers.*

1. As you listen to the lecture, decide whether each of these traits has a negative (−) or a positive (+) correlation to heart disease. Mark each with the correct sign, − or +.

   _____ a. bacteria and viruses

   _____ b. hardening of the arteries

   _____ c. cigarette smoking

   _____ d. regular physical activity

   _____ e. being overweight

   _____ f. anxiety

   _____ g. creativity

_____ h. being a woman

_____ i. urbanization

_____ j. traditional society

_____ k. stress

_____ l. adrenaline and noradrenaline

2. As you listen to the lecture, write *Bert* or *Adam* or *both* next to each description.

_____ a. He is married and has children.

_____ b. His professional life is not easy for him.

_____ c. He doesn't mind waiting for people.

_____ d. He has a close relationship with his family.

_____ e. He is probably overweight.

_____ f. He has fewer hobbies now than he used to have.

_____ g. Work is not his only interest.

_____ h. He is not very religious.

_____ i. He doesn't have very much self-confidence.

_____ j. He is his own worst enemy.

The Mechanics of a Heart Attack

In order to understand heart disease, it is necessary to study the heart itself, its parts, and its needs. Every heart is divided into four parts, or chambers (see Figure 16). It is symmetrical — that is, the right half looks like the left half. The upper chambers are used for holding or collecting blood for short periods of time. They are called auricles. The lower chambers are used for *pumping* blood out of the heart. They are called ventricles. The right side of the heart has the job of pumping blood to the lungs so that the blood can obtain oxygen. The left side of the heart receives this oxygen-rich blood and pumps it through *vessels* called arteries.

Some of this blood goes back into the heart itself. The heart needs oxygen and *nourishment* from the blood to do its very important work. Without oxygen, the heart muscle cannot live for more than a few seconds. If for some reason the heart does not receive fresh blood, that part of the heart muscle will die almost immediately. This is precisely what happens in a heart attack. Therefore,

Figure 16. The heart and its parts.

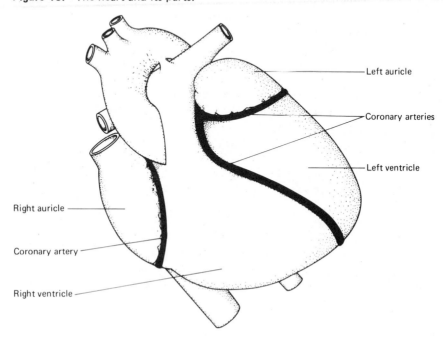

Left auricle

Coronary arteries

Left ventricle

Right auricle

Coronary artery

Right ventricle

the first job in preventing heart attacks is to make sure that the heart receives nourishment and oxygen for its work.

Exactly how does the heart muscle receive fresh blood? The main artery leaving the heart is the vessel for all the body's fresh blood. Five percent of the blood going into this artery is taken back into the heart muscle itself, to nourish the heart. A system of two main arteries, called the coronary arteries, leaves directly from this main artery. The coronary arteries travel around the heart, dividing into smaller and smaller vessels, until every bit of heart muscle is supplied with blood. If the heart is to be healthy, these arteries must be healthy. They must do their job well and allow plenty of life-supporting blood to pass through.

The immediate cause of heart disease is coronary artery disease. If these arteries do not allow enough blood to flow through, then the heart itself is in very serious danger. The first sign of coronary artery disease is a slow process which takes months, years, and even decades. It is called arteriosclerosis, or "hardening of the arteries."

This is how arteriosclerosis works. First the lining of the artery receives small wounds, or injuries, caused by the *twisting* of the heart muscle. Wounds may also be caused by high blood pressure, or by some *substance* in the blood, such as strong hormones. Next the artery produces a patch of cells around this wound as it tries to *heal* itself. Now the real problem may begin. A fatty substance in the blood, called cholesterol, may begin to collect around this patch of cells. Eventually a kind of *tumor* is formed; this tumor growth is called a plaque.

Plaques are dangerous for two reasons. First, they narrow the artery so that it is partially blocked. Second, and far more dangerous, the plaques can themselves die and break open. Large blood clots in the coronary arteries may result. A blood clot that is large enough can completely close the coronary arteries.

This, then, is the immediate cause of a heart attack. When portions of plaque break off, large clots can completely close the coronary artery and prevent the nourishment of a part of the heart muscle. Part of the heart muscle receives no oxygen for a few minutes, and it dies. The pain, shortness of breath, and general *distress* of the patient are great. Almost half of the *victims* of heart attacks die very soon after this happens. The *survivors* find that their heart is weakened to some degree, making some changes in their life necessary. They may experience shortness of breath, inability to exercise, and some irregularities in their heartbeat. If the same process of cholesterol buildup is not prevented in the future, half of these people will experience another attack within five years.

pump   to send a liquid or gas by force through tubes or pipes

vessel   a container; in this case, like a tube

nourishment   material necessary for life or growth

twist   turn

substance   material, matter

heal   repair, make well

tumor   a growth that comes from existing tissue; it grows independently and doesn't perform any job for the body

distress   suffering

victim   someone who is hurt, harmed, or killed

survivor   a person who continues to live

Comprehension Questions

1. Write a good definition for each of the following words. You should be able to do this by using only the information contained in the article.

   chamber

   symmetrical

   auricle

   ventricle

   heart attack

   coronary artery

   arteriosclerosis

   cholesterol

   plaque

2. What job do the auricles of the heart perform? What job do the ventricles perform?

3. Where does blood go before the heart pumps it out into the rest of the body?

4. What happens when the heart muscle does not receive fresh blood?

5. What job do the coronary arteries perform?

6. Why are plaques dangerous?

7. What are the results of a heart attack?

8. What can be done to prevent hardening of the arteries?

LISTENING TEST: CHANGING FROM TYPE A TO TYPE B BEHAVIOR

Incomplete Outline

Directions: *Read the outline before you listen to the lecture, so you will know what kinds of things you need to listen for. While you are listening, find the missing phrases to complete the outline. Use abbreviations wherever possible. Mark your paper while you listen.*

I. Can a Type A personality change?

   A. A person can change his behavior.

   B. It is never too late.

II. Behavioral change program

   A. Understanding oneself

      1. Introspection is painful for the Type A person because

         _____ .

      2. Type A people measure their value by _____

         _____ .

      3. Real knowledge of oneself promotes _____

         _____ .

   B. Exploring all the areas of one's personality

      1. Type A people are interested in _____ .

      2. Benefits of hobbies

         a. _____

b. _____

c. _____

C. Specific exercises to change behavior
    from Type A   to Type B

    1. Use of time

       _____   _____

       _____   _____

       _____   _____

    2. Waiting

       _____   _____

       _____   _____

       _____   _____

    3. Hostility

       _____   _____

       _____   _____

       _____   _____

    4. Positive emotions

       _____   _____

       _____   _____

       _____   _____

True-False Questions

1.   6.
2.   7.
3.   8.
4.   9.
5.   10.

Cultural Change:
The Anasazi

INTRODUCTION TO THE LECTURE

Topic: The Story of the Anasazi

One of the many different American Indian cultures is that of the Pueblo Indian tribe in the Southwest. The Pueblo Indians are a major American tribe that has lived by farming for almost 2000 years. One early branch of the Pueblo tribe lived from 1 A.D. to 1300 A.D. in the Four Corners area, where the states of Colorado, Utah, Arizona, and New Mexico meet. These prehistoric Indians were called the Anasazi. We have been able to follow their development by studying changes in their baskets, pots, and houses. This lecture tells how their culture developed, flourished, and then changed.

Thesis: Cultural Change

All cultures change, even modern ones. By studying the history of an older culture such as that of the Anasazi, we can see how change works. The introduction or invention of one new feature (such as pottery) can eventually have an important effect on the entire culture (its diet, its housing, and its wealth).

Figure 17. The Four Corners area.

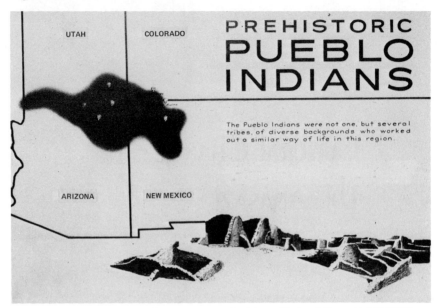

Photograph by Patricia Wilcox Peterson, courtesy of Aztec National Monument Museum.

Organizational Strategy: Chronological Order

The lecturer describes Anasazi culture in four time periods.

    I. Introduction
   II. Early Basketmaker period
  III. Modified Basketmaker period
  IV. Developmental Pueblo period
   V. Classic Pueblo period

BASIC SENTENCES

Directions: *Together the basic sentences provide a short summary of the main ideas in the lecture. Read and study these sentences before you listen to the lecture for the first time.*

Introduction

1. The American Indians of the Southwest have led an agricultural life since the year 1 A.D., and in some aspects their life is still similar today.

2. The most critical and influential improvement in their lives was the use of containers to cook, store, and carry their food and water.

3. We classify the four time periods of their history like this: first, Early Basketmaker; second, Modified Basketmaker; third, Developmental Pueblo; and fourth, Classic Pueblo.

Early Basketmaker

4. Probably in the summertime they lived on the mesa top near their fields, in temporary structures made of poles and brush.

5. In winter they most likely moved down to the caves in the cliffs for warmth and protection against the snow.

6. Baskets were used for carrying things, for storing corn, and even for carrying water and cooking food.

7. The Early Basketmakers simply couldn't make food that needed to cook slowly all day, such as beans, soups, or stews.

Figure 18. Early Basketmaker life.

Photograph by Stuart Wier, courtesy of Mesa Verde National Park Museum.

Figure 19. Modified Basketmaker house.

Photograph by Stuart Wier, courtesy of Mesa Verde National Park Museum.

Modified Basketmaker

8. The new type of house was a permanent structure of mud and poles, built on the mesa top.

9. Pottery was the most important addition to Modified Basketmaker life.

10. Because the Anasazi had solved the problem of cooking and storing food, they could now enjoy a more prosperous, comfortable period of life.

Figure 20. Basketry.

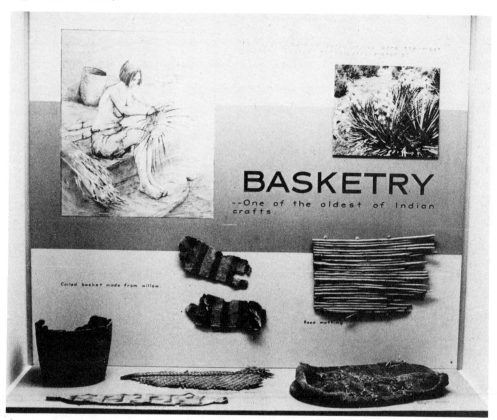

Photograph by Patricia Wilcox Peterson, courtesy of Aztec National Monument Museum.

Developmental Pueblo

11. The earlier pit houses were modified to one-story row houses, made with pieces of stone.
12. Several separate buildings stood near each other like a small village.

Figure 21. Modified Basketmaker pots.

Figure 22. Developmental Pueblo houses.

Photographs by Stuart Wier, courtesy of Mesa Verde National Park Museum.

Figure 23. A mesa.

Photograph by Patricia Wilcox Peterson.

Classic Pueblo

13. In spite of advanced cultural development, the Classic Pueblo era was a sad time: It marked the end of the Anasazi civilization in this area.

14. The Indians moved back down to the caves in the cliffs where they had spent winters a thousand years before.

15. The final problem might have been enemy attack, sickness, lack of rain, or overfarmed soil.

Figure 24. Corrugated cooking pot.

Photograph by Patricia Wilcox Peterson, courtesy of Aztec
National Monument Museum.

Figure 25. Classic Pueblo houses.

Photograph by Stuart Wier, courtesy of Mesa Verde National Park Museum.

Figure 26 (a). Dishes, bowls, mug, and storage jug.

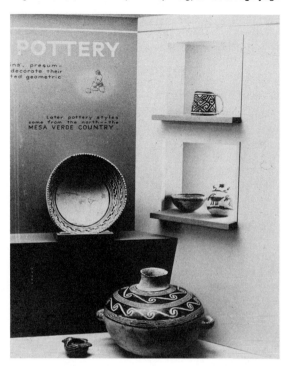

Figure 26 (b). Ladles.

Photographs by Patricia Wilcox Peterson, courtesy of Aztec
National Monument Museum.

ADDITIONAL VOCABULARY

Directions: *Below are some additional words that may be new to you. Look up the ones you don't know before listening to the lecture.*

ancient	flourish	nomadic
clay	Great Plains	nuts
corn	jug	prehistoric
cradleboard	ladle	sandals
descendants	mug	squash
		yucca fibers

Listening Cues: Vocabulary of Chronological Order

Directions: *Below are some important words and terms that point out chronological development in the lecture. Learn the meanings of any phrases you don't already know. As you listen to the lecture, these words will help you understand the relationship of different ideas to one another.*

at the beginning	later	first
in their early history	eventually	second
_____ years before	the last	third
before _____	the end	fourth
		next
still	from the year _____	then
today	to the year _____	final, finally
now	since the year	
during	_____	
no longer	for _____ years	
again	around the year	
still again	_____	
by this time		

STUDY SKILLS

Note-Taking Practice: Abbreviations

As you listen to the lecture, you may want to use abbreviations for some of the more common words and phrases. Here are some suggestions.

Specialized words which appear often in this lecture:

Early Basketmaker	EB	modern	mod
Modified Basketmaker	MB	cultures	cult
Developmental Pueblo	DP	mountain	mt
Classic Pueblo	CP	basket	bas
Southwest	SW	pottery	pot
American Indians	Amer Ind	development	dev
		binding material	bind mat

Words that appear in many academic lectures:

and	+, &	small	sm
important	imp	large	lg
addition	+	geometric	geom

Exercise One: Rephrasing Sentences for Note-Taking

Directions: *Listen to the following sentences as your teacher reads them. Often you can tell which words are most important by the stress and volume of a person's voice. Key words are stressed and spoken more loudly. Write the words you think are most important in the space below each sentence. Feel free to use abbreviations and mathematical symbols. The first example is done for you.*

1. At the beginning of this period, the people farmed on the tops of high, flat mountain plateaus called *mesas*.

   Farming on mt. plateaus (mesas)

2. *Mesa* is the Spanish word for *table*.

   _____

3. They lived on the top of the mesas or in the protection of caves in the sides of the cliffs.

   _____

4. The first period, Early Basketmaker, lasted until 450 A.D.

   _____

5. They made fine, strong sandals for their feet and soft, sturdy cradleboards for their babies.

   _____

6. The first attempt at pottery came as women mixed clay — a kind of dirt — with water to make pots.

   _____

7. The change from basketmaking to pottery was so important that it began a series of secondary changes.

   _____

8. Some villages were as large as several hundred rooms and could contain as many as 1,000 people.

   _____

Name: _____ Date: _____ **125**

9. The name for this kind of house and for these Indians is *Pueblo*, which is the Spanish word for *village*.

_____

10. Around the year 1300, all the people suddenly left their homes and moved far away.

_____

Exercise Two: Recognizing the Main Idea

Directions: *Read these paragraphs from the lecture, or ask your teacher to read them to you. Then decide what topic heading you would use to describe the main idea of each. Write the topic heading above each paragraph.*

1. *Cultural change* _____

    All cultures change, even modern ones. As a matter of fact, change occurs most rapidly in modern cultures, since science brings us so many new discoveries every day. It is rather difficult to follow these changes clearly because they happen so fast. Older, more stable civilizations are easier to observe.

2. _____

    There are four different time periods in the development of the Anasazi. Scientists have looked for one most important theme in this story, a kind of unifying idea to organize all the facts. The most influential part of the Anasazi's lives was the way they used containers, so this is the way we classify their development.

3. _____

    The houses they lived in were not meant to be permanent dwellings; as a matter of fact, we have no remaining evidence of their houses. Probably in the summertime they lived on the mesa top near their fields. In winter they most likely moved down to the caves in the cliffs for warmth and protection against the snow.

4. _____

    The most important job of the man in this society was to learn, teach, and perform the religious ceremonies associated with farming. Women wove baskets out of yucca fibers; they also worked in the fields and prepared all the food.

5. _____

The pots the women made this way were far superior to baskets for carrying, cooking, and storing food and water. Now the people could add beans, a rich source of protein, to their diet. Water could be stored safely over long periods. Life became much easier, and so effort could now be spent on other developments.

6. _____

We don't know what the final problem was. It might have been enemy attack, sickness, lack of rain, or overfarmed soil. But in the year 1300, the last of the Anasazi left the cliff dwellings, never to return. They left behind their beautiful pueblos, which still stand as a monument to them.

7. _____

No formal history was written for these early Indians, but Navajo Indians who came along later found evidence of their great civilization. The Navajos called these prehistoric people "the Anasazi," which means "the ancient ones."

8. _____

Descendants of the Anasazi still live in the Southwest, and many aspects of their culture are the same as they were in ancient times. Today these people are called Pueblo Indians.

INCOMPLETE OUTLINE

Directions: *Read the outline before you listen to the lecture for the first time, so you will know what kinds of things you need to listen for. While you are listening, find the missing dates and phrases to complete the outline. Use abbreviations wherever possible. Mark your paper while you listen.*

    I. Introduction

        A. Cultural change

            1. Change occurs rapidly in _____.

2. Other civilizations are easier to observe, such as that

   of _____.

B. Civilization in the Four Corners area (_____-

   _____ A.D.)

   1. Farming on _____ _____.

   2. Around 1300, _____.

   3. Navajos called the Indians the Anasazi, which means

      "_____."

   4. Anasazi development is divided into four time periods,

      organized by _____ _____

      _____.

      a. In their early history, the Anasazi used _____.

      b. Later they developed _____.

II. _____ period (_____-_____

    A.D.)

A. Before this period, the Anasazi were _____

   _____ in the _____
   area.

B. Housing — not permanent

   1. Summer: _____

   2. Winter: _____

C. Diet

    1. _____

    2. _____

    3. _____

D. Basketmaking with yucca fibers

    1. Women made baskets, _____ , and _____.
    2. Uses

        a. _____

        b. _____

        c. _____

        d. _____

    3. Disadvantages of cooking in baskets

        a. The process was _____.

        b. There was a limited amount of _____ in the
            diet.

III. _____ period (_____ - _____
    A.D.)

A. Housing — permanent

    1. Houses were made of _____.
    2. Indians lived on mesa tops all year long.

B. Pottery

    1. Men brought home _____ but not

    _____.

Name: _____ Date: _____ **129**

2. People experimented with different methods.

    a. Clay + _____ = _____ .

    b. Clay + _____ = _____

    _____ .

    c. Clay + _____ = _____ .

3. Advantages of pottery

    a. People added _____ to their diet.

    b. _____ could be stored safely.

    c. Easier life allowed _____ .

IV. _____ period (_____ - _____ A.D.) (best period)

  A. Housing

    1. Pit houses were modified to _____ .

    2. Several separate buildings formed _____

    (Spanish name = _____ = " _____ ").

  B. Pottery

    1. It had _____ designs.

    2. Anasazi used bowls, _____ , and

    _____ .

    3. Pottery replaced _____ .

V. _____ period (_____ – _____
   A.D.)

   A. Pottery

      1. It was finely decorated.

      2. _____ was decorated with a corrugated, textured design.

   B. Housing shows end of Anasazi civilization in Mesa Verde area

      1. 1100–1200: _____

         a. _____

         b. _____

      2. 1200: _____

         _____

      3. 1300: _____

         _____

         a. _____

         b. _____

         c. _____

         d. _____

WORD RECOGNITION EXERCISE

Directions: *Fill the blanks in each word family by finding the missing parts of speech in your dictionary. Divide each word into syllables and mark the syllable that takes primary stress, as shown.*

Word Families

Noun	Verb	Adjective	Adverb
1. ú ni ty	——————	——————	XXXXXXX
2. ——————	——————	in flu én tial	XXXXXXX
3. ——————	ac cul´tur ate	——————	——————
4. dwell´ing	——————	XXXXXXX	XXXXXXX
5. ——————	mod´i fy	——————	XXXXXXX
6. so cí e ty	XXXXXXX	——————	XXXXXXX
7. ——————	——————	——————	ad di´tion al ly
8. ——————	——————	ex per i mén tal	——————
9. ——————	——————	dú ra ble	——————
10. ——————	——————	——————	e láb o rate ly
11. ——————	de fend´	——————	——————
12. ——————	as só ci ate	——————	XXXXXXX
13. ——————	——————	re fléc tive	——————
14. ——————	clas´ si fy	——————	XXXXXXX
15. ——————	crit´i cize	——————	——————

MAKING NEW WORDS

Directions: *The prefix* pre *means* before. *Add the prefix* pre *to each of the adjectives below. Tell what each new word means and use it in a sentence.*

historic   *prehistoric*   *before history was recorded*

Navajo Indians found evidence of this prehistoric civilization.

scientific   _____   _____

_____

technological   _____   _____

_____

agricultural   _____   _____

_____

modern   _____   _____

_____

TRUE-FALSE EXERCISE

Directions: *Read these sentences before you listen to the lecture for the second time. While you are listening, decide whether each item is true or false. Mark your paper with a T for true or an F for false while you listen.*

_____ 1. Change occurs most rapidly in prehistoric cultures.

_____ 2. The American Indians of the Southwest have changed their way of life completely in the past 2,000 years.

Name: _____ Date: _____   **133**

_____ 3. The Anasazi lived on the mesa tops before the Navajo Indians came to that area.

_____ 4. The change from basketmaking to pottery was a secondary change.

_____ 5. The Early Basketmakers' temporary houses reflected their earlier wandering habits.

_____ 6. The Early Basketmakers moved down to caves in the cliffs for protection against their enemies.

_____ 7. The Early Basketmakers cooked their food in baskets by placing the baskets on top of hot stones.

_____ 8. Men from a hunting or trading party saw pottery in another Indian village and realized immediately how to make it.

_____ 9. Clay bound together with grass and straw is not very hard or durable.

_____ 10. In the Developmental Pueblo period, the Anasazi culture developed to its height.

_____ 11. Some Developmental Pueblo villages were as large as several hundred rooms and could contain as many as 1,000 people.

_____ 12. During the first half of the Classic Pueblo period, the people continued to live on the mesa tops.

_____ 13. Around the year 1200, the Indians began to spend winters in the caves in the cliffs.

_____ 14. Life in the cliffs was less crowded and more comfortable than on the mesa tops.

_____ 15. We don't know whether the Indians moved away because of natural disasters or enemy attack.

TOPICS FOR DISCUSSION AND WRITING

1. Although the Anasazi men brought home the idea of pottery, they did not bring home any instructions on how to make it. List the steps in the process the women followed to invent pottery for themselves.

2. Besides baskets, the Early Basketmakers also made other things from yucca fibers. However, by the time of the Developmental Pueblo period, basketmaking was a lost art. Can you think of a negative effect (a loss to the culture) that came about through the change to pottery?

3. Cultural anthropologists have defined three different kinds of cultural change in a society:

   Invention — the creation of a new object or process by one or more persons

   Innovation — the adaptation and refinement of an object or process that already exists

   Borrowing — the transference and adoption of an object or process from one culture by another

   Can you think of an example of each from Anasazi history?

4. Anthropologists still argue about the reason the Anasazi left the Four Corners area. There are four main theories, and each has some supporting evidence. Match each theory with the evidence to support it.

Theory	Supporting Evidence
Enemy attack	The Anasazi had planted the same fields for 1300 years.
Sickness	The cliff dwellings were crowded, damp, and filled with smoke.
Lack of rain	Pueblo houses reflected a growing concern with defense.
Overfarmed soil	There was practically no rain in the Mesa Verde area from the year 1276 to the year 1300.

5. In which of these cultures would change come more quickly? In which culture would change be easier to observe and understand? Give reasons.

   The United States since 1945

   The Pueblo Indians from 1 A.D. to 1300 A.D.

---

6. The lecturer clearly states that "the change from basketmaking to pottery was so important that it began a series of secondary changes." We know that pottery solved the problem of storing and cooking food, so that life became much easier for the Anasazi after its introduction to their culture.

   a. Name some secondary changes that came after the shift to pottery.

   b. Why was the Developmental Pueblo period a time of so much innovation, while the Early Basketmaker period was quite static by contrast?

   c. What simple requirements must be fulfilled before people's energy can be freed for thought and invention?

   d. The lecturer does not state her views about the relative importance of various human needs. But she does *imply* something about this. Which of these needs would she probably say are most important? Number the needs from most important to least important.

   Warm housing

   Fresh water

   Food

   Extra time for relaxation and thought

   Religious traditions

7. In many countries there is one dominant culture, which uses the official language of the country; in addition, there are various subcultures with their own languages and traditions. Describe this kind of situation in a country other than the United States. Be sure to mention ways in which the two cultures influence each other.

8. Do you think that cultural change occurs more quickly in times of peace or in times of war? Give examples to support your opinion.

9. The Anasazi were skilled at crafts, as we can see from their fine baskets and pots. Describe some of the traditional crafts from other countries.

10. It has been said that technical development and true progress are not always the same thing. As countries develop and enter the modern world, there can be disadvantages as well as advantages. As new ways are accepted, old ways disappear. Tell about the advantages and disadvantages of development in a country you know.

MULTIPLE CHOICE EXERCISE

Directions: *Choose the one answer that best completes each sentence. Write the letter of the correct answer in the blank.*

_____ 1. Descendants of the Anasazi
   a. live in Mesa Verde.
   b. live in pueblos.
   c. are called Navajos.
   d. a and b.

_____ 2. The most important change in Anasazi development was
   a. the move from basketmaking to pottery.
   b. the move from caves to pit houses.
   c. the move from pit houses to pueblos.
   d. the move away from Mesa Verde.

_____ 3. The Early Basketmakers were like nomadic hunters because
   a. they didn't want to carry heavy pots with them.
   b. they didn't eat meat.
   c. they didn't build permanent houses.
   d. all the above.

_____ 4. Anasazi women were responsible for
   a. working in the fields and making baskets or pots.
   b. teaching religion and preparing food.
   c. trading and hunting.
   d. a and b.

_____ 5. In Anasazi development there were modifications of
   a. houses.
   b. containers.
   c. diet.
   d. all the above.

_____ 6. The Developmental Pueblo Indians lived in houses
   a. in the caves in the cliffs.
   b. made of brush and poles on the mesa tops.
   c. made of mud and poles on the mesa tops.
   d. made of pieces of stone.

_____ 7. If you were making a pot, what would you need?
   a. clay and water
   b. grass and bark
   c. sand and a hot fire
   d. a and c

Name: _____   Date: _____

8. Classic Pueblo Indians used
   a. mugs, ladles, and jugs.
   b. tableware with black and white designs
   c. cookware with a corrugated, textured design.
   d. all the above.

9. The Anasazi moved into cliff dwellings around 1200 because
   a. winters were too cold on the mesa tops.
   b. life was less crowded in the caves.
   c. somebody was threatening them on the mesa tops.
   d. they needed more room for their crops.

10. Implied, but not stated, in the lecture is the idea that
    a. basic needs must be met before a culture can flourish.
    b. the Basketmakers were not an inventive people.
    c. the change from basketmaking to pottery was so important that it began a series of secondary changes.
    d. the Classic Pueblo period was the best period of Anasazi history.

FINAL LISTENING ASSIGNMENT: NOTE-TAKING

Directions: *Read these questions before you listen to the lecture for the third time. While you are listening, write the answers. You may use abbreviations if you want to.*

1. What were the social roles of men and women in Anasazi culture? (What jobs did each do?)

2. The Early Basketmakers dug shallow storage pits for their corn. How did this idea develop in the Modified Basketmaker period?

3. How did the introduction of pottery improve Anasazi life?

4. How were Developmental Pueblo houses different from Basketmaker houses?

5. Describe three ways the Classic Pueblo Indians changed their houses and living patterns to provide better defense.

Discovering the Anasazi

Dozens of Anasazi families had already left the mesa by 1299, but the tribe's final departure was sudden. Little food was left, and almost no water. Every winter the people had hoped for snow, and every spring they had prayed for the rain that never came. It had been this way for twenty-four years: a dry period that weakened the strong and killed the weak. Finally the thing happened that people had feared most — the only corn that was left was their seed corn. They did not dare eat that, for then they could never be farmers again. They had to take their seed corn and leave the mesa for a better home.

In their hurry to be gone, they left everything as it was. Perhaps they felt that everything in the pueblos was unlucky; perhaps they were trying to escape the evil *spirits* of the mesa. Cooking pots and work tools lay there, ready to use, as if the people intended to return soon. But nobody came back.

Figure 27. Cliff Palace.

Photograph by Stuart Wier.

Soon after they left, the weather changed, and the rain returned. The mesa became green and rich again. People wandered back over the mesa tops; this time they were Navajo Indians. As they discovered the incredible *ruins*, they stood *amazed*. Afraid of the spirits in these houses, the Navajos decided not to live there. But from this time, the Indians knew of the cliff dwellings. They spoke about the people who had made them, calling them the "Ancient Ones."

Centuries passed, and the cliff dwellings stood untouched by human beings. The sweeping winds of the mesa blew into the caves and covered the cooking pots and work tools with the dry dust of the Southwest.

Across the oceans, the great nations of Europe were beginning to look to the New World for gold and for land. England, Spain, and France sent their soldiers, priests, and explorers. Slowly they approached the mesa. First to see the large mesa were the Spanish, who gave it its name: Mesa Verde — green table.

Pioneers of the young nation, the United States, were next to command the area. They drove back the Spanish and made a kind of peace with the Indians of the region, the Utes. But none of the newcomers wanted to try farming there, for there was not much rain. *Cattle* raising became the main occupation around Mesa Verde.

The Wetherill family was friendly with the Ute Indians, and from the Utes they may have heard stories of mysterious houses in the *cliffs*. To show their friendship, the Utes permitted the Wetherills to keep their cattle on Indian land during the winter. The cowboys gathered their cattle together again in the spring.

This is how, in the spring of 1888, Richard Wetherill and his cousin Charlie Mason came to be on the mesa. Following the tracks of a few lost cattle, they rode to the top of the mesa. They had just come to the edge of a cliff when they paused to rest their horses. Where were the cattle? They looked down into the *canyon* below — and up again to the top of the neighboring cliff.

Then suddenly, Wetherill forgot completely about his cattle as he discovered something fantastic! Was it real? How could there be — here in the middle of the lonely mesa — an entire city of perfectly fitted stone blocks, built to hold hundreds of people in its graceful towers and square rooms? And where were the people who had built such a wonder? Wetherill decided that the city was suitable for a king and his family, and he called it Cliff Palace.

Wetherill's discovery changed his whole life. Before the discovery, he had been a cowboy with no advanced education. But because he was a sensitive man, he realized how important his discovery was. Wetherill made two promises to himself: he must discover everything he could about the people who had lived here, and he must protect the ruins for the future. He spent the rest of his life keeping these promises.

Wetherill's situation was not well suited to the job, and he had little support from the general public or the academic world. Still, he invested the small income from his farm in exploratory trips to the ruins. Because his ranch demanded his time during the summer, he had to wait until the cold winters to explore the cliffs. He rose at dawn, dug and searched all day, and then spent the dark evening hours recording his discoveries. He did not want anything to be lost or misplaced. He made careful records of all the pots, tools, and jewelry.

Wetherill's collection of museum pieces would have made the most scholarly archeologist proud. He found 182 different cliff dwellings in the Mesa Verde area, and he was also the first to discover evidence of the Basketmakers. He realized that there must have been an earlier people who had come before the Pueblo Indians. When he announced his theories and findings to the world, the university arthropologists and archeologists simply laughed at him. Without even investigating, they refused to believe him!

But the patient Wetherill continued to work and to record his discoveries. Almost ten years after his death, scientists discovered evidence of the Basketmakers for themselves and proved that he had been right. Now a large part of Mesa Verde National Park bears his name: Wetherill Mesa. And so the ruins, which for many years stood quietly unexplored, were finally discovered and preserved. Wetherill was a man very much like the cliff dwellings themselves — quiet, strong, and enduring. He belonged to the area and he brought out one of its greatest secrets.

---

spirit a ghost of a dead person

ruins the remains of something which has been destroyed

amazed very surprised

cattle cows

cliff the steep rocky side of a mountain

canyon a deep, narrow gap in the earth's surface with cliff walls on both sides

Comprehension Questions

1. What reasons have been given to explain why the Anasazi left their homes?

2. Did they take everything with them? How do we know?

3. Who lived in Mesa Verde after the Anasazi?

4. How did Richard Wetherill discover Cliff Palace?

5. How did this discovery change his life?

6. What characteristics did Richard Wetherill have that suited him to explore the cliff dwellings?

7. To whom does Mesa Verde belong now?

8. Tell the origin of these names: Anasazi, Mesa Verde, Cliff Palace.

SPEAKING ACTIVITY: ROLE PLAYING

Directions: *Each member of the class should choose to play the part of one of the people listed below. As a homework assignment before class, prepare answers to the questions about the person you have chosen. In class, each person can tell his or her story.*

Anasazi Priest (The spiritual and political leader of the Anasazi)

1. What happened during the 24-year period before you took your people off the mesa?
2. What did you do to try to bring rain?
3. When did you decide that your only choice was to leave?
4. Why did your people leave their cooking pots and work tools in the cliff houses?
5. Soon after your people left, the rains came. What is your explanation for this?
6. Did you have any trouble keeping your position as leader after this disaster?

Navajo Wanderer

1. When did you discover the cliff dwellings?
2. What did you think about their origin?
3. What did you call the people who made them?
4. Why didn't you move in and live in the cliff dwellings?

Spanish Explorer

1. Who was living on the mesa when you saw it?
2. Why did you name it Mesa Verde?
3. Did you see any cliff dwellings?
4. What made you leave the Mesa Verde area?
5. What other Spanish influences besides the name *Mesa Verde* remain in the American Southwest?

Ute Indians

1. When did you discover the cliff dwellings in Mesa Verde?
2. Did you live in the cliff dwellings?
3. Were you friendly with any of the cowboys around Mesa Verde? What did you do for the Wetherills?
4. Did you tell anybody about the cliff dwellings?

Richard Wetherill

1. What is your educational background and occupation?
2. Where do you live?
3. How did you come to be on Mesa Verde in the spring of 1888?
4. Please describe the mesa.
5. What did you see on Mesa Verde? How did you feel?
6. Did you make any decisions or promises to yourself when you saw the Cliff Palace?
7. Did you receive any help from anthropologists?
8. How and when did you explore the mesa?
9. What theory or discovery was your most important?
10. Have you received any reward for your work?

Anthropologists

1. What did you think at first of Richard Wetherill?
2. Why didn't you help him?
3. What kind of collection did Richard Wetherill gather?
4. What was your reaction to Wetherill's theory about the Basket-makers?
5. How do you feel about Wetherill now?

LISTENING TEST: THE ANTHROPOLOGIST'S TOOLS

Incomplete Outline

I. Introduction: Three ways to learn about the Anasazi civilization

    A. Observing the Anasazi's modern descendants — the Pueblo Indians

        1. They are living examples of _____.

        2. They have a rich oral tradition of _____.

    B. Written reports by Spanish explorers and soldiers

        1. They recorded their observations _____.

        2. There was little culture change except for _____

        _____.

    C. Examining physical evidence from the Anasazi

        1. Ways to read the evidence

            a. Study _____.

                (1) This tells _____.

                (2) Example: _____.

b. Look at _____ .

    (1) Newer objects are _____ and

    older objects are _____ .

    (2) Objects in the same layer are _____

_____ .

II. Physical objects can tell about the way of life

  A. Change in head shape from _____ to _____
     A.D.

    1. At the beginning of the period _____

_____ .

    2. By the end of the period _____

_____ .

  B. Scientists at first thought _____ .

    1. Intermarriage could produce _____

_____ .

    2. Culture change would explain _____

_____ .

  C. Additional physical evidence produced a new theory

    1. Archeologists found cradleboards that are _____

_____

_____.

  a. The earlier cradleboard was _____.

  b. The later cradleboard was _____.

2. The result of the change in cradleboards was _____

_____.

3. Scientists concluded that _____

_____.

True-False Questions

1.	6.
2.	7.
3.	8.
4.	9.
5.	10.

Outlines with a Student's Responses

LANDSATS: HOPE OF THE FUTURE

Incomplete Outline

This is an example of one student's work on the incomplete outline. Notice the use of abbreviations. Compare his answers with yours.

I. Introduction

II. What are Landsats?

    A. Two butterfly-shaped spacecraft sent into orbit in

        _1972_ and _1975_.

    B. They circle the earth _14_ times every

        _24_ hours.

    C. They photograph every part of the earth every

        _9_ days.

    D. Each picture covers an area of about _100_ square miles.

III. How do Landsats work?

   A. A photo is printed from black-and-white negatives through color filters to produce a false-color picture.

      1. Water is _black_.

      2. _Rock_ is brown.

      3. Healthy plants are _red_.

      4. Diseased plants are _green_.

   B. Scientists base their interpretations on the patterns of the colors.

IV. How can Landsats be used?

   A. The first important use is to create better _maps_.

   B. The second use is to find _oil and minerals_.

   C. Another use is to find _fresh water_.

   D. The fourth use is to _watch crops growing_.

   E. The fifth use is to _warn us of natural disasters_.

   F. Some other uses are:

      1. To find _large schools of fish in the oceans_

      2. To show where _pollution is greatest_

      3. To provide a record of _how the population is growing_

V. What are the future plans for Landsats?

   A. Another Landsat will measure _heat_.

   B. Other Landsats may be equipped with _radar_.

C. Other countries that will receive Landsat data are:

1. Canada
2. Brazil
3. Italy

4. *Iran*
5. Zaire

6. *Chile*

SOLAR ENERGY: AN ENERGY ALTERNATIVE

Incomplete Outline

This is an example of one student's work on the incomplete outline. Notice the use of abbreviations. Compare his answers with yours.

I. Introduction: The need for new energy sources

   A. For the last ___50___ years, oil has been an inexpensive source of energy.

   B. Oil may be a major source of energy for only ___25___ more years.

II. Other sources of energy available to us

   A. Coal

   1. Advantage: We have a lot.
   2. Disadvantages: There may be problems with

      mining it, *transporting* it, and developing a way to *burn* it without polluting the air.

   B. Nuclear energy

   1. Advantage: We have enough uranium for a long time.

2. Disadvantages: Public concern over the *safety* of nuclear energy. The government once thought we would be getting *20* % of our electricity from nuclear energy by the *1970's*, but nuclear energy produced only about *12* % as of 1979.

C. Solar energy (from Latin *sol*, meaning *sun*)
   1. Advantages

      a. It is clean and unlimited.

      b. The amount falling on the U.S. is *700* times our total energy consumption.

      c. By 2000, it could supply *25* % of our energy needs.

   2. Disadvantage: The cost of converting sunshine to solar energy is high.

III. The solar heating of buildings
  A. Advantages
    1. It is cheaper than gas or oil.

      a. There is no need to purchase *fuel*.

      b. Little or no *maintenance* is necessary.

    2. It can be used almost anywhere.
  B. Disadvantages
    1. Purchase cost

      a. The cost for a three-bedroom house is

      $7,000 to $12,000.

b. This is a _one-time_ cost that can be financed over many years.

2. Additional cost — alternate heating system

   a. Solar systems can't always provide _100_ % of your heat.

   b. You must have a _gas_, _oil_, or _electric_ furnace.

C. How solar heating works (hot-air and hot-liquid)

   1. Parts

      a. _collector_

      b. _storage unit_

      c. _thermostat_

      d. _auxiliary heating unit_

   2. Hot-air system

      a. The collector catches the _sun's rays_.

      b. The sun heats the _panels_.

      c. The panels heat the _air inside_.

      d. On sunny days when heat is needed, hot air flows to the thermostat, into the _heating system_, and back to the collector.

      e. On sunny days when heat is not needed, hot air flows to the thermostat, then into

      a storage unit.

f. At night, the thermostat sends air from the

__storage___ __unit_____ into the building.

3. Hot-liquid system

a. It contains __water_____ instead of air.

b. The storage unit is _a hot-water tank._

BARTER: AN OLD IDEA WITH NEW POWER

Incomplete Outline

*This is an example of one student's work on the incomplete outline.
Notice the use of abbreviations. Compare his answers with yours.*

I. Trading and the market system

    A. Trading without money (barter)

*the process of trading by exchanging goods for
other goods; ex. seashells ↔ spices, no*

    B. The evolution to a monetized society *specified value*

*Some societies today not monetized -insignifi-
cant amt. of trade. Interim: both systems*

    C. Trading with money *together ex. seashells ↔ spices
↔ money*

*Each nation prints own money, with spec
value Money = exchange medium*

II. Barter in the modern world

    A. Reasons for barter

        1. Types of currency

a. Hard = _more valuable, in higher demand, particularly by seller_

b. Soft = _less valuable, difficult to trade_

2. Inflation = _abnormally high rate at which prices rise; erodes purchasing power of hard currency_

B. Examples

1. Countries with no precise figures available

   a. _Eastern European communist countries_

   b. _Africa_

   c. _Asia_

   d. _Latin America_

2. Reasons why it is difficult to give examples

   a. _Terms of contract are not disclosed_

   b. _So that competitors will not come in_

3. Examples with public attention

   a. _Beverages in USSR, US — Pepsi-cola, vodka_

   b. _Western Eur. autos, Eastern Eur. apricots (Problem finding a market for the apricots)_

YOUR PERSONALITY AND YOUR HEART

Incomplete Outline

This is an example of one student's work on the incomplete outline. Notice the use of abbreviations. Compare his answers with yours.

I. Introduction

    A. If stress and time pressure make you nervous

        1. *your pers type = the maj of am.*

        2. *your pers may be killing you*

    B. Heart disease in the United States — like an epidemic

        1. *h.d. = epidemic · 1000's die / year*

        2. *h.d. ≠ earlier epidemics, not ← virus or bacteria*

II. Cause of heart disease

    A. Immediate cause — arteriosclerosis and cholesterol buildup

        1. What *→ art* ?

        2. Why *to some people, not others* ?

    B. Companions to heart disease   Relationship to heart disease

        1. *Fat and chol. in diet*   *pos. cor. c̄ h.d.*

        2. *Cig smoking*   *not primary cause*

        3. *Phys inactivity*   *not predictors*

        4. *Being overweight*   *not in every h.d. victim*

        5. *High b.p.*   *catalyst once process begun*

    C. First causes of arteriosclerosis and cholesterol buildup

        1. Personality Type A

            a. Traits: *anxious, nervous, competitive, set goals, meet deadlines, irritable, hostile, less creative*

b. Where we find Type A people: _50-60%, all levels of society, more ♂ than ♀, inc. c̄ modern life, younger than before (40-60)_

2. Physical mechanism connecting brain and heart

a. Effects of stress

1. _Chol in blood rises_

2. _high b. p._

3. _hormone inc - adrenaline, noradrenaline_

4. _Clotting factor speeds_

b. Research shows _high cor. of h.d. & pers. A_

III. Contrast Type A (Adam)   and   Type B (Bert)

will develop h.d. by 60   won't develop h.d. before 70

A. Similarities

1. Family life: _married, children, 50 +_

2. Professional life: _successful in work, but professions not easy_

B. Differences

1. View of life: _tension,   life enjoyable_
   hostility

2. Use of time: _fights time, resents waiting, works every minute_   _sets fewer tasks, entertains himself while waiting_

3. Social habits: _not a good observer or listener, no friends_   _good listener, strong friendships_

4. Physical activity: _no time to exercise, drives car_   _regular exercise, enjoys playing, is thin_

5. Relaxation: _few hobbies, brings work home with him_   _3 or 4 hobbies, forgets work when at home_

6. Spiritual life: _both not religious, but belong to a church_
no self-confidence, not a thinker or problem solver, compulsive, repetitive activity, Life is useless, pointless   _peace of mind, balance in life, Puts work troubles out of his mind until he finds a creative solution, confidence, self-respect_

IV. Change in behavior pattern → chance for a healthy life
(value of training Type A individuals in Type B behavior)

A. _More valuable than other therapy_

B. _Spiritual and psychological benefit_

REWRITTEN LECTURE NOTES

I. Introduction

A. If stress and time pressure make you nervous

1. Your personality type is like that of the majority of Americans.

2. Your personality may be killing you.

B. Heart disease in the United States — like an epidemic

   1. Heart disease is like an epidemic, in that thousands die from it every year.
   2. Heart disease is unlike earlier epidemics, in that it is not caused by virus or bacteria.

II. Cause of heart disease

A. Immediate cause — arteriosclerosis and cholesterol buildup

   1. What causes arteriosclerosis?
   2. Why does is happen to some people, but not to others?

B. Companions to heart disease	Relationship to heart disease
1. Fat and cholesterol in diet 2. Cigarette smoking 3. Physical inactivity 4. Being overweight 5. High blood pressure	These have a positive correlation to heart disease, but they are not the primary cause of heart disease. They won't predict who will have heart disease, nor are they present in every victim. Once the process has begun, they act as catalysts.

C. First cause of arteriosclerosis and cholesterol buildup

   1. Personality Type A

      a. Traits: anxious, nervous, competitive, set high goals, meet deadlines, irritable, hostile, less creative, acting under stress
      b. Where we find Type A people: 50 to 60% of all Americans today, at all levels of society, more men than women, increasing Type A behavior with modern life, younger men than before (age 40 to 60)

   2. Physical mechanism connecting brain and heart

      a. Effects of stress

         1. Cholesterol in blood rises
         2. High blood pressure
         3. Hormone levels in blood increase — adrenaline, noradrenaline

4. Hormones speed the clotting time of the blood

    b. Research shows a high correlation of personality Type A with heart disease.

III. Contrast Type A (Adam)   and   Type B (Bert)

Adam will develop heart disease by the age of 60.	Bert won't develop heart disease, at least not before age 70.

A. Similarities

    1. Family life: Both are married, have grown children, and are over 50.
    2. Professional life: Both have been successful in their work, but their professions are not easy.

B. Differences

    1. View of life

        a. Adam is full of tension and hostility toward life.
        b. Bert finds life enjoyable.

    2. Use of time

        a. Adam fights time, resents waiting, and works every minute.
        b. Bert sets himself fewer tasks and entertains himself while waiting.

    3. Social habits

        a. Adam is not a good observer or listener. He has few friends.
        b. Bert is a good listener and forms strong friendships.

    4. Physical activity

        a. Adam has no time to exercise, always drives a car, and lacks the peace of mind that exercise can give.
        b. Bert exercises regularly, enjoys playing games, and is healthy.

    5. Relaxation

        a. Adam has few hobbies and brings his work home with him.
        b. Bert has three or four hobbies and forgets his work when he is at home.

    6. Spiritual life: Neither man is religious, but both belong to a church.

a. Adam has no self-confidence, is not a thinker or a problem-solver. He is trapped in compulsive, repetitive activity. He feels that life is useless and pointless.
b. Bert enjoys peace of mind and a balanced life. He puts work troubles out of his mind when he is at home and often finds that he can think of creative solutions later. He has self-confidence and self-respect.

IV. Change in behavior pattern → chance for a healthy life (value of training Type A individuals in Type B behavior)

  A. Behavior training can be more valuable than other forms of therapy.

  B. A change in lifestyle brings spiritual and psychological benefit as well as physical improvement.

CULTURAL CHANGE: THE ANASAZI

Incomplete Outline

This is an example of one student's work on the incomplete outline. Notice the use of abbreviations. Compare his answers with yours.

I. Introduction

  A. Cultural change

    1. Change occurs rapidly in *mod cult*.

    2. Other civilizations are easier to observe, such as that

    of *amer Ind of SW*.

  B. Civilization in the Four Corners area (*___/___* -

    1300 A.D.)

    1. Farming on *flat mt plateau - mesa (table)*

    2. Around 1300, *people moved away*.

3. Navajos called the Indians the Anasazi, which means

"_the ancient Ones_,"

4. Anasazi development is divided into four time periods,

organized by _how_ _used_

containers.

    a. In their early history, the Anasazi used _bas_.

    b. Later they developed _pot_.

II. _EB_ period (_1_ – _450_ A.D.)

A. Before this period, the Anasazi were _nomadic hunters_

in the _Great Plains_ area.

B. Housing — not permanent

    1. Summer: _mesa top, near fields, poles & brush_

    2. Winter: _caves in cliff_

C. Diet

    1. _corn_

    2. _squash_

    3. _nuts_

D. Basketmaking with yucca fibers

    1. Women made baskets, _sandals_ and

cradleboards.

2. Uses

    a. _carry things_

    b. _store corn_

    c. _carry water_

    d. _cook food_

3. Disadvantages of cooking in baskets

    a. The process was _long, burned fingers_
    b. There was a limited amount of

    protein in the diet.

III. _m β_ period (_450_ - _750_ A.D.)

A. Housing — permanent

    1. Houses were made of _mud o poles, mesa tops (started c̄ holes like pits in floor, then built up_
    2. Indians lived on mesa tops all year long.

B. Pottery _most imp addition_

    1. Men brought home _idea_ but not

    instructions.

    2. People experimented with different methods.

    a. Clay + _water_ = _dried, crumbled_.

    b. Clay + _grass, straw, bark_ = _held together until on fire; bind mat burned → holes_.

    c. Clay + _sand (baking)_ = _successful, hard, durable_

3. Advantages of pottery

    a. People added *beans (protein)* to their diet.

    b. *Water* could be stored safely.

    c. Easier life allowed *other dev*.

IV. *D P* period (*750* - *1100* A.D.) (best period)

  A. Housing — permanent

    1. Pit houses were modified to *1- story row houses*, *stone*

    2. Several separate buildings formed *sm village →* *1000 pop*

    (Spanish name = *pueblo* = " *village* ").

  B. Pottery

    1. It had *black & white geom* designs.

    2. Anasazi used bowls, *mugs, ladles*, and *jugs*.

    3. Replaced *bas*.

V. *C P* period (*1100* - *1300* A.D.) (a sad time!)

  A. Pottery

    1. It was finely decorated.

    2. *Cookware* was decorated with a corrugated, textured design. *(pinching wet clay)*

  B. Housing shows end of Anasazi civilization in Mesa Verde area.

1. 1100–1200: _Concern with defense_ { _closer_ _tall_ _towers_

    a. _other tribes_

    b. _other Pueblo Indians_

2. 1200: _moved back to caves, Pueblo in caves_

3. 1300: _Anasazi left_

    a. _enemy ?_

    b. _sick ?_

    c. _rain ?_

    d. _soil ?_

REWRITTEN LECTURE NOTES

I. Introduction

   A. Cultural change

      1. Change occurs rapidly in modern cultures.
      2. Other civilizations are easier to observe, such as that of the American Indians of the Southwest.

   B. Civilization in the Four Corners area (1–1300 A.D.)

      1. Farming on flat mountain plateaus called mesas (Spanish-table).
      2. Around 1300, the people moved away.
      3. Navajos called the Indians the Anasazi, which means "the Ancient Ones."
      4. Anasazi development is divided into four time periods, organized by how they used containers

a. In their early history, the Anasazi used baskets.
b. Later they developed pottery.

II. Early Basketmaker period (1–450 A.D.)

A. Before this period, they were nomadic hunters in the Great Plains area.
B. Housing — not permanent

    1. In the summer, they lived on the mesa tops near their fields, in houses of poles and brush.
    2. In the winter they lived in caves in the cliffs, and used storage pits for corn.

C. Diet: corn, squash, and nuts
D. Basketmaking with yucca fibers

    1. Women made baskets, sandals, and cradleboards.
    2. Uses

        a. Carrying things
        b. Storing corn
        c. Carrying water
        d. Cooking food

    3. Disadvantages of cooking in baskets

        a. The process was long and it burned fingers.
        b. There was a limited amount of protein in the diet.

III. Modified Basketmaker period (450–750 A.D.)

A. Housing — permanent

    1. Houses were made of mud and poles, and built on the mesa tops. They started with a hole in the floor like a storage pit, and then built up.
    2. Indians lived on mesa tops all year long.

B. Pottery — the most important addition

    1. Men brought home the idea, but not instructions on how to make it.
    2. People experimented with different methods.

        a. Clay and water — when dry, it crumbled and fell apart.
        b. Clay and grass, straw, or bark — when on the fire, the binding material burned up and left holes.
        c. Clay and sand, baked pots — successful, very hard and durable.

3. Advantages of pottery

    a. People added beans (protein) to their diet.
    b. Water could be stored safely.
    c. Easier life allowed effort to be spent on other developments.

IV. Developmental Pueblo period (750–1100 A.D.) (best period)

  A. Housing

    1. Pit houses were modified to one-story row houses of stone.
    2. Several separate buildings formed a small village of as many as 1,000 people (Spanish name-pueblo-village).

  B. Pottery

    1. It had black and white geometric designs.
    2. Anasazi used mugs, ladles, bowls, and storage jugs.
    3. Pottery replaced basketry.

V. Classic Pueblo period (1100–1300 A.D.) (a sad time)

  A. Pottery

    1. It was finely decorated.
    2. Cookware was decorated with a corrugated, textured surface, made by pinching the wet clay with the fingers.

  B. Housing shows end of Anasazi civilization in the Mesa Verde area

    1. 1100–1200: The villages reflected a concern for defense. They were built closer together, with tall towers for protection.

      a. Threat of other tribes?
      b. Threat of other Pueblo Indians?

    2. 1200: The Indians moved back to caves in the cliffs, and built pueblos there.
    3. 1300: The Anasazi left the cliff dwellings.

      a. Enemy attack?
      b. Sickness?
      c. Lack of rain?
      d. Overfarmed soil?

BiblioqRAphy

Carroll, John B., "Defining Comprehension: Some Speculations," Educational Testing Service, Princeton, N.J., 1971.

Carroll, John B., "Some Suggestions from a Psycholinguist," *TESOL Quarterly*, (1973), Vol. 7, No. 4, 355–367.

Friedman, Meyer, and Ray Rosenman, *Type A Behavior and your Heart*, Alfred A. Knopf, New York, 1974.

Quinn, Terence, and James Wheeler, "Listening Comprehension in the Foreign Language Classroom," CAL/ERIC/C11 Series on Languages and Linguistics, No. 16 (1975), 38 pgs.

Rivers, Wilga, "Listening Comprehension," *Modern Language Journal*, Vol. 50, No. 4, (1966), 196–204.

_____ , "Search for the Ancient Ones: For Richard Wetherill, the Discovery of Mesa Verde was Only the Beginning," *Colorful Colorado*, Vol. X, No. 4, Jan/Feb. 1975.

Wilson, *Let's Try Barter*, The Devin-Adair Co., New York, 1960.